Wild Roses

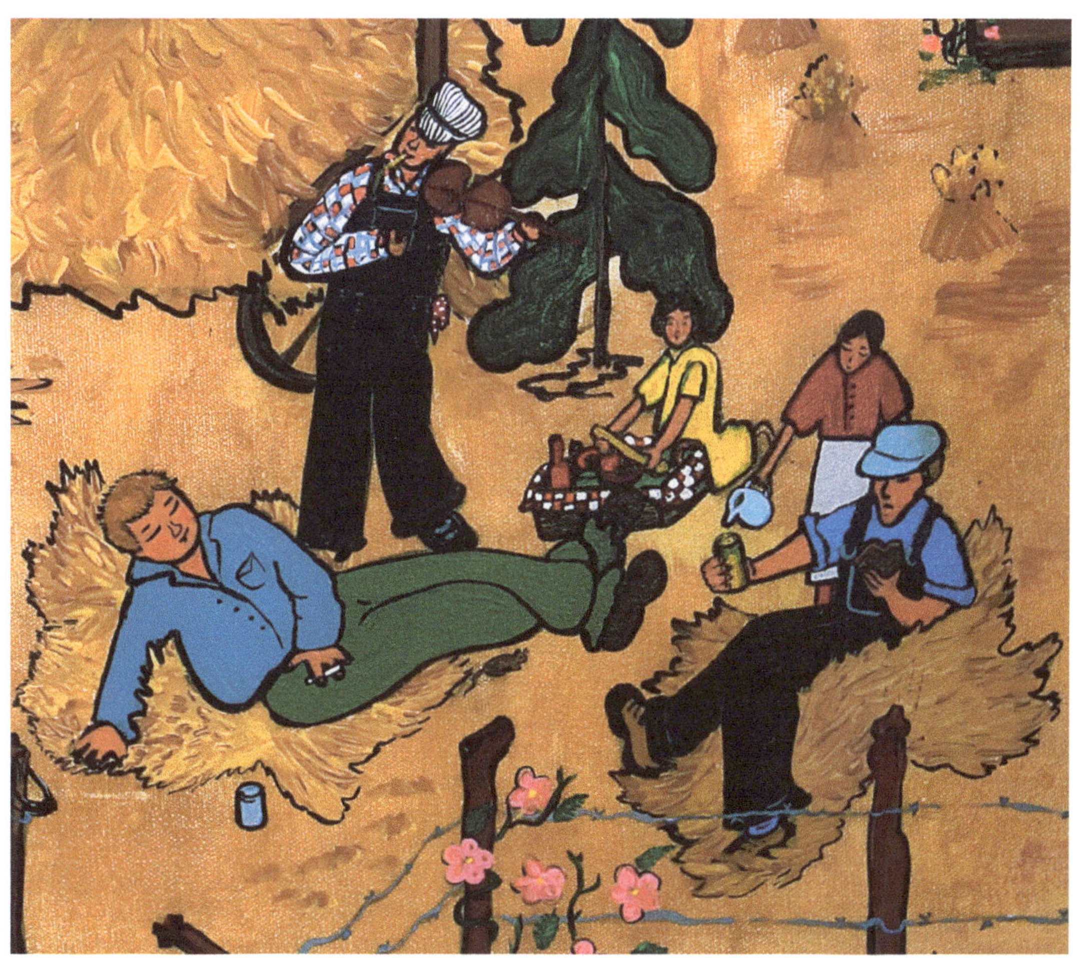

Homestead Memories [detail]

In memory of our Andy, who said to me,
"Mom, your work always touches my heart."

And for all my children who daily touch my heart:

Zoe and Leon
Randi
Paige
Danté
Heidi, Mark and Hayden.

To my Tom, who forever encourages me;
to my friends, you know who you are;
and to my readers: May my work touch your hearts as it did Andy's.

With thanks to G. Harry Brown and Myles Lamont for their wonderful photos of my art and to all the folks at Hancock House Publishers whose patience and sense of humor made getting Wild Roses *into print a wonderful experience.*

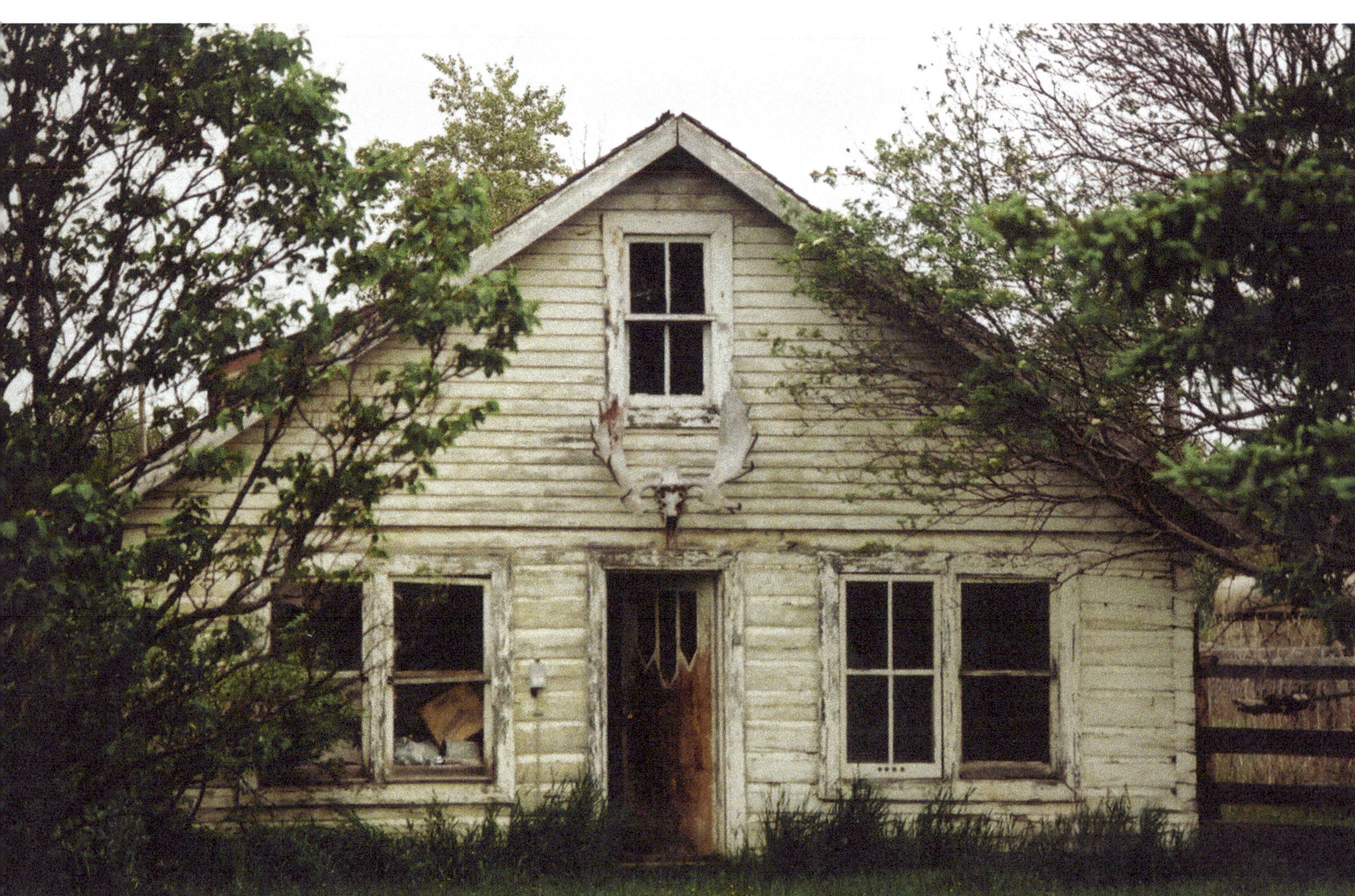

Our "new" house on the farm, built when I was five to seven years old. Dad hand cut and hued every log by himself.

Wild Roses

Memories of a Homesteader's Daughter

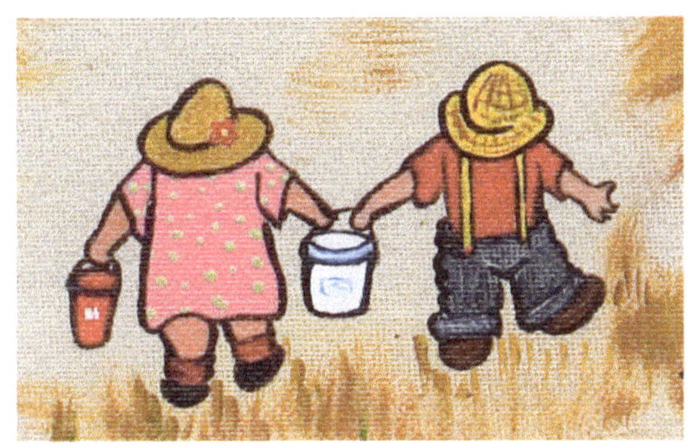

Stories & Artwork by
dutchie Rutledge-Mathison

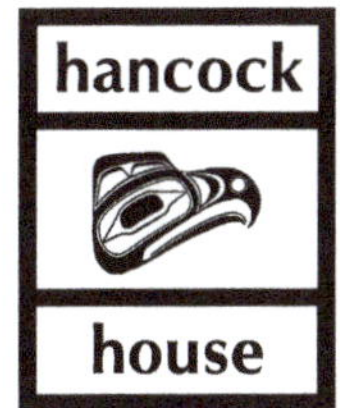

ISBN-10: 0-88839-625-2
ISBN-13: 978-0-88839-625-9

Cataloguing in Publication Data

Rutledge-Mathison, Dutchie, 1938–
Wild roses : memories of a homesteader's daughter / dutchie Rutledge-Mathison.

ISBN 0-88839-625-2

1. Rutledge-Mathison, Dutchie, 1938– 2. Frontier and pioneer life — Alberta, Northern — Pictorial works. 3. Alberta, Northern — Biography. I. Title.

FC3694.25.R87 2006 971.23'02092 C2006-904479-1

Printed in the USA

Editor: Theresa Laviolette
Cover Design: Laura Michaels
Production: Laura Michaels, Ingrid Luters
Photography: G. Harry Brown, Myles Lamont

We acknowledge the financial support of the Government of Canada through the Book Publishing Industry Development Program (BPIDP) for our publishing activities.

Published simultaneously in Canada and the United States by

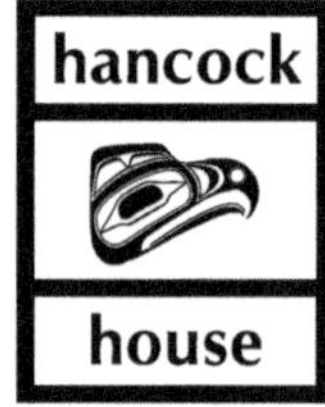

HANCOCK HOUSE PUBLISHERS LTD.
19313 Zero Avenue, Surrey, B.C. Canada V3Z 9R9
(800) 938-1114 Fax (800) 983-2262
www.hancockhouse.com
info@hancockhouse.com

Contents

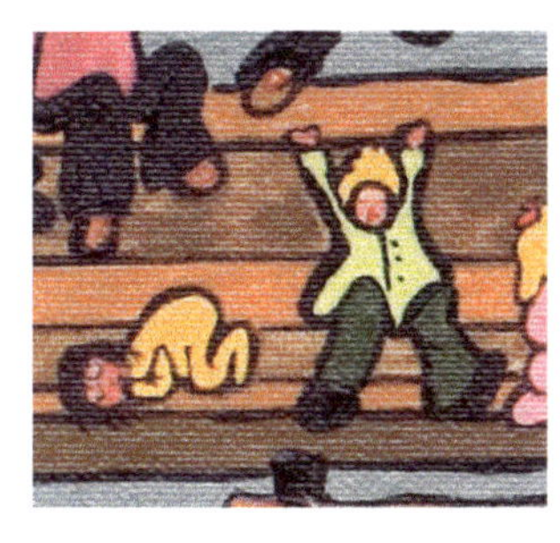

Prologue 6
1 Thirties 8
2 Twins 10
3 Red Shoes 12
4 Long Walk 14
5 Trap Line 16
6 Lesson 19
7 Chores 22
8 Stampede 24
9 Potato. 27
10 Hay 30
11 Sheep 32
12 Saskatoons 34
13 Sandhills. 36
14 Winter Wood 38
15 Dad's Cows 42
16 Storyteller 44
17 Prairie Chickens 48
18 Sawmill. 50
19 Mother's Child 52
20 Mabel's Baby 54
21 Mom's Bedroom. 56
22 Ukrainian 60
Conclusion 67
Epilogue 71

Prologue

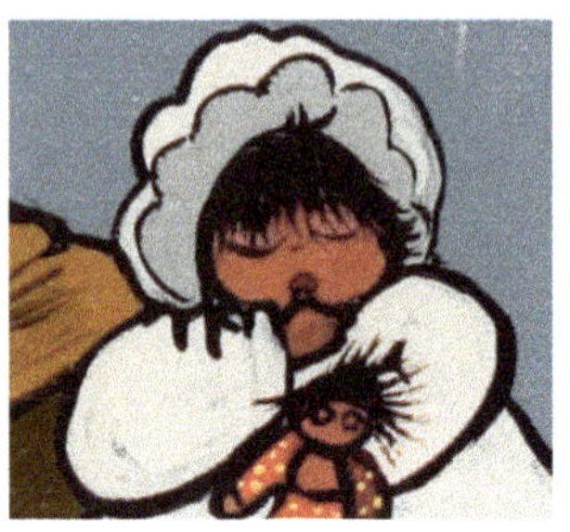

We moved recently, my husband and I, from our large family home to a townhouse. Better, we told each other, less work for older bodies. More time for my passion, painting. A good decision, I knew. Then why did it seem so bittersweet?

The housewares were packed into boxes and labeled. Extra furniture was divided among the children. An easy task, done quickly without sentiment. Then I came to the sideboard, my storehouse for decades of photographs and family snapshots. Some neatly titled and dated, most stuffed into old shoeboxes in complete disregard of time or place. First our family pictures — babies, tots to teenagers, on to family weddings and new babies, tots, and teenagers. My life cycle lay exposed; not to be denied, but cherished with memories of what seemed only yesterday.

I sifted through until I came to a box of my mother's memories. Boxes I had stored after we lost her; rarely opened because they saddened my happy, active life.

With trepidation I opened the first album, small sepia pictures labeled and four cornered onto black pages. Through tears I relived each picture that reflected her youth. Then, I came to a small snap after she had married my father. She was standing with a group of women holding babies while toddlers clung shyly to their skirts. She was pregnant, holding my eldest sister so I knew she was only in her mid twenties. They were "old" these women, aged by too many children, hard work, and isolation. I quickly put the albums away. Packing left little time for tears.

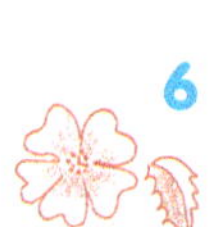

Once moved and into my brand new studio, the lighting perfect, my brushes clean: a new canvas lay stretched and waiting for a story. My fingers followed the images of my mind, back to my mother and the other young women in the valley. I painted *The Immigrants* and a new series, *The Homesteaders*, was born.

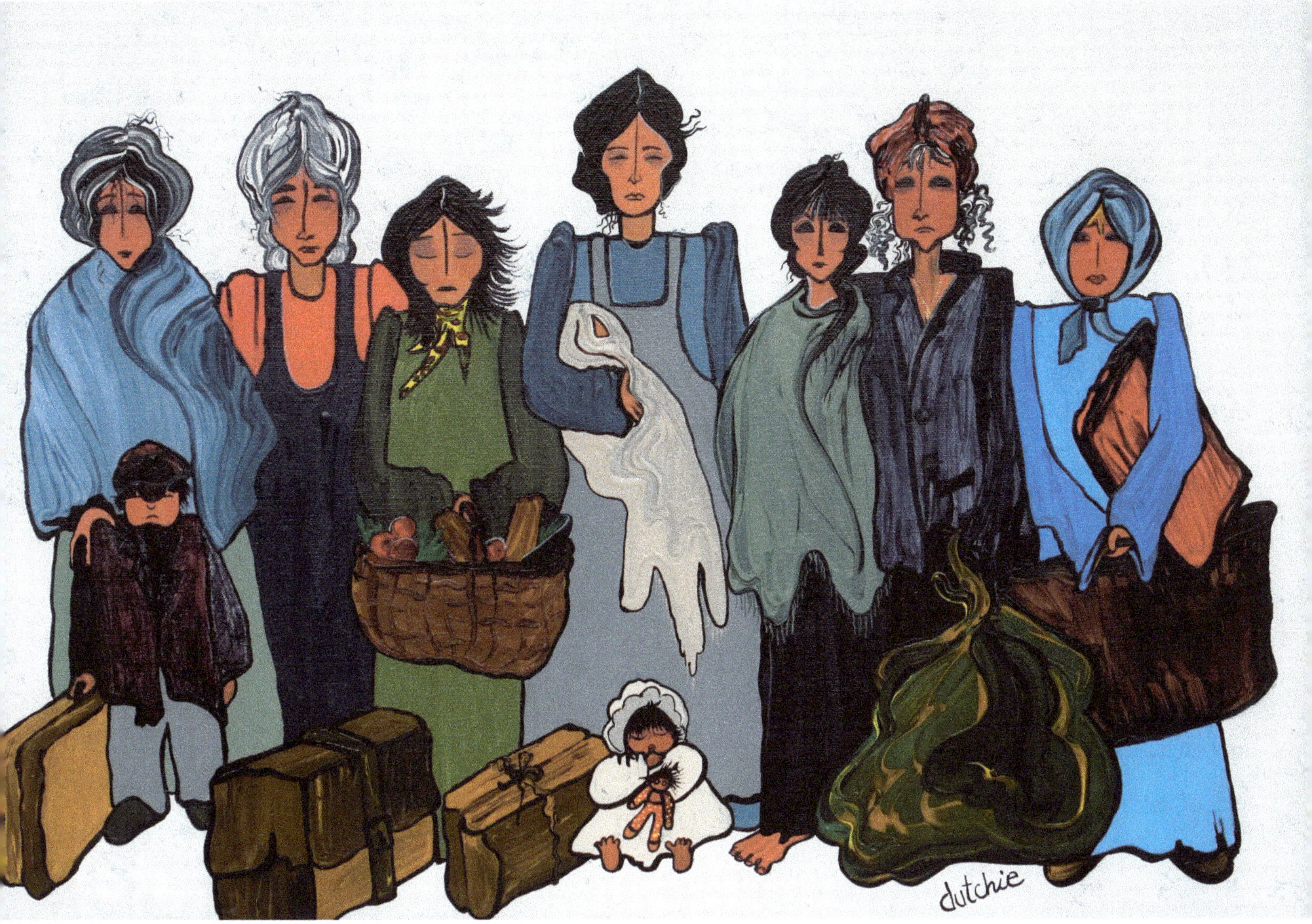

The Immigrants
acrylic / canvas
65 x 42 cm

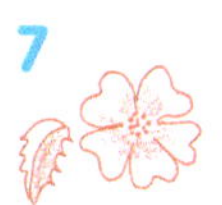

1 Thirties

In the 1930s the area around Lesser Slave Lake included several small villages of 100–200 souls and thousands of acres of virgin crown land designated for homesteads. My parents staked claim to 160 acres south of Lesser Slave Lake, deep in the valley of the Swan River and seven miles from the nearest town. There, like the earlier settlers of eastern Canada, they struggled as a family to improve their land and eke out a living.

The majority of their fellow homesteaders hailed from Great Britain, Europe, and the Balkan area of Eastern Europe, the United States, and Russia. My father, who was of Irish descent, came "riding the rails." Simply put, he jumped on a slow train and ignored the fare. He had no particular destination in mind. The train stopped at Kinuso, filled its boilers with water, and steamed away without Dad. He found a job and decided the valley was where he wanted to stake his claim on a homestead site, improve his land, and raise a family.

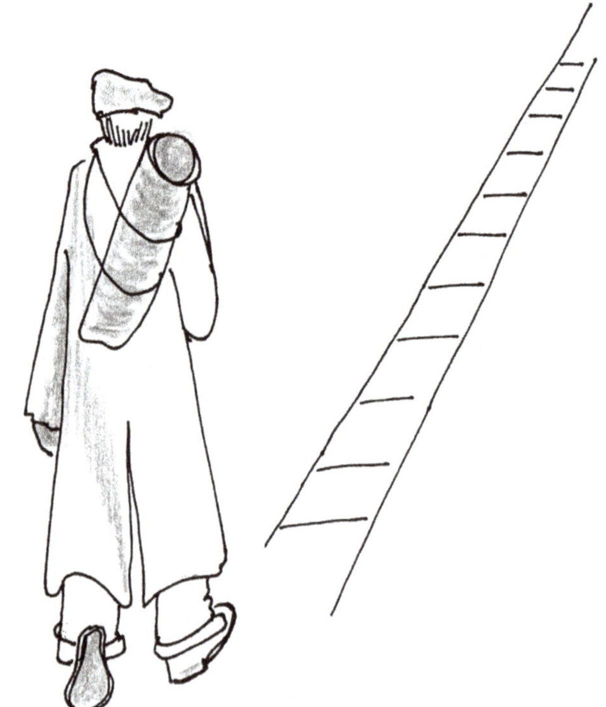

My mother, who was born in the US, came from southern Alberta with her family. They were headed for the Peace River Country, advertised by the Canadian government as the last of the best homestead area in Canada. Their plans changed when snow arrived early. They decided to spend the winter in the valley.

My parents married in 1934 and worked their valley homestead together for nearly twenty years. My grandparents stayed in Kinuso until returning "home" to the eastern United States over two decades later.

My father, as he aged, often spoke of the day he filed for his homestead. Apparently the nearest land office was in the town of High Prairie, some sixty miles west of the valley. His only source of transportation was, again, a free ride on a slow train.

His claim staked, my dad attempted to board his transportation home when a young RCMP officer stopped him and informed him that he could not allow him to take his illegal ride. As he walked away the officer turned and with a grin said, "I do believe the train slows for a corner about a mile east of town."

Dad said his legs were already heading east as the Mountie got on his horse and rode off.

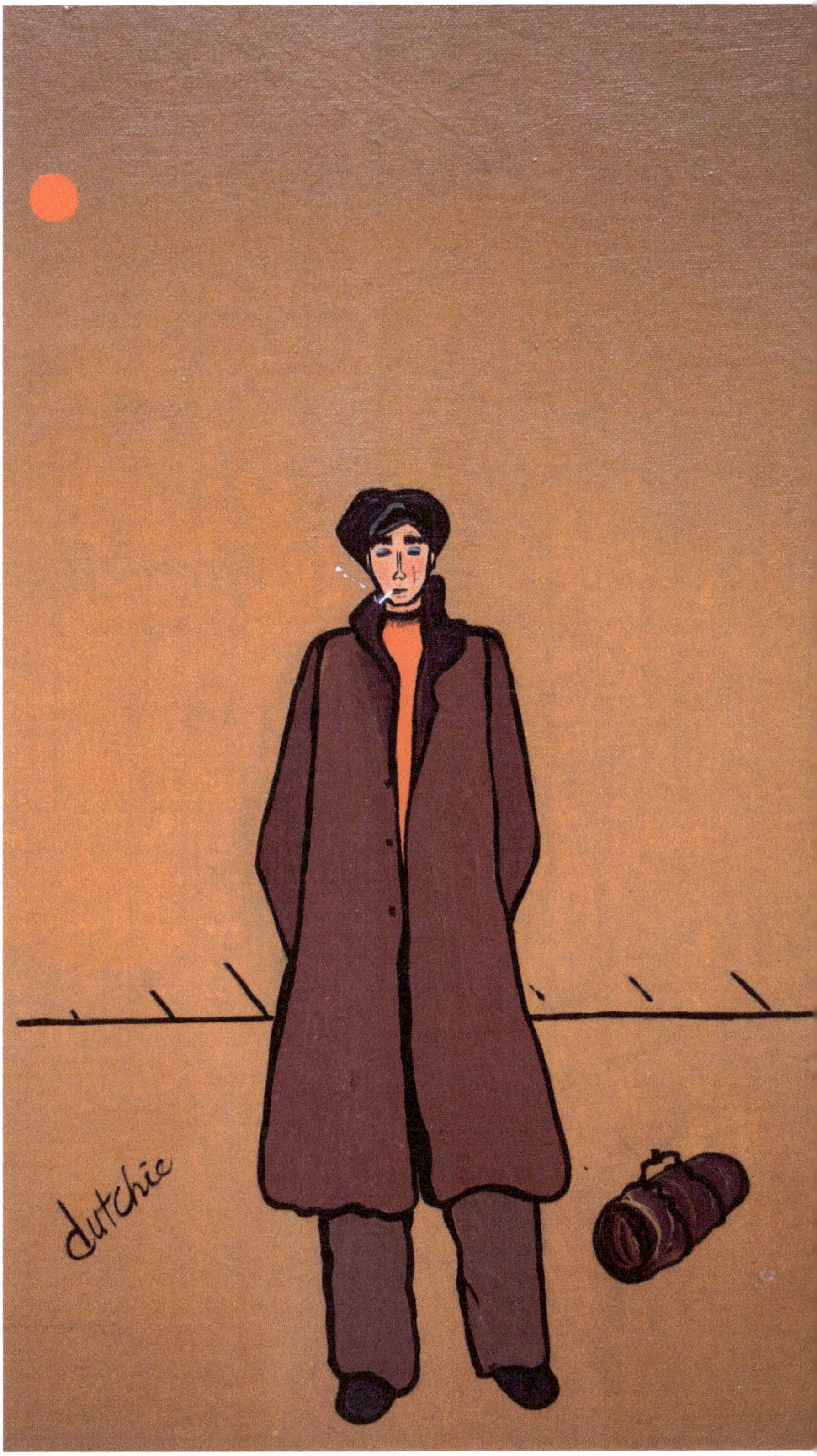

Dad

acrylic / canvas

60 x 45 cm

2 Twins

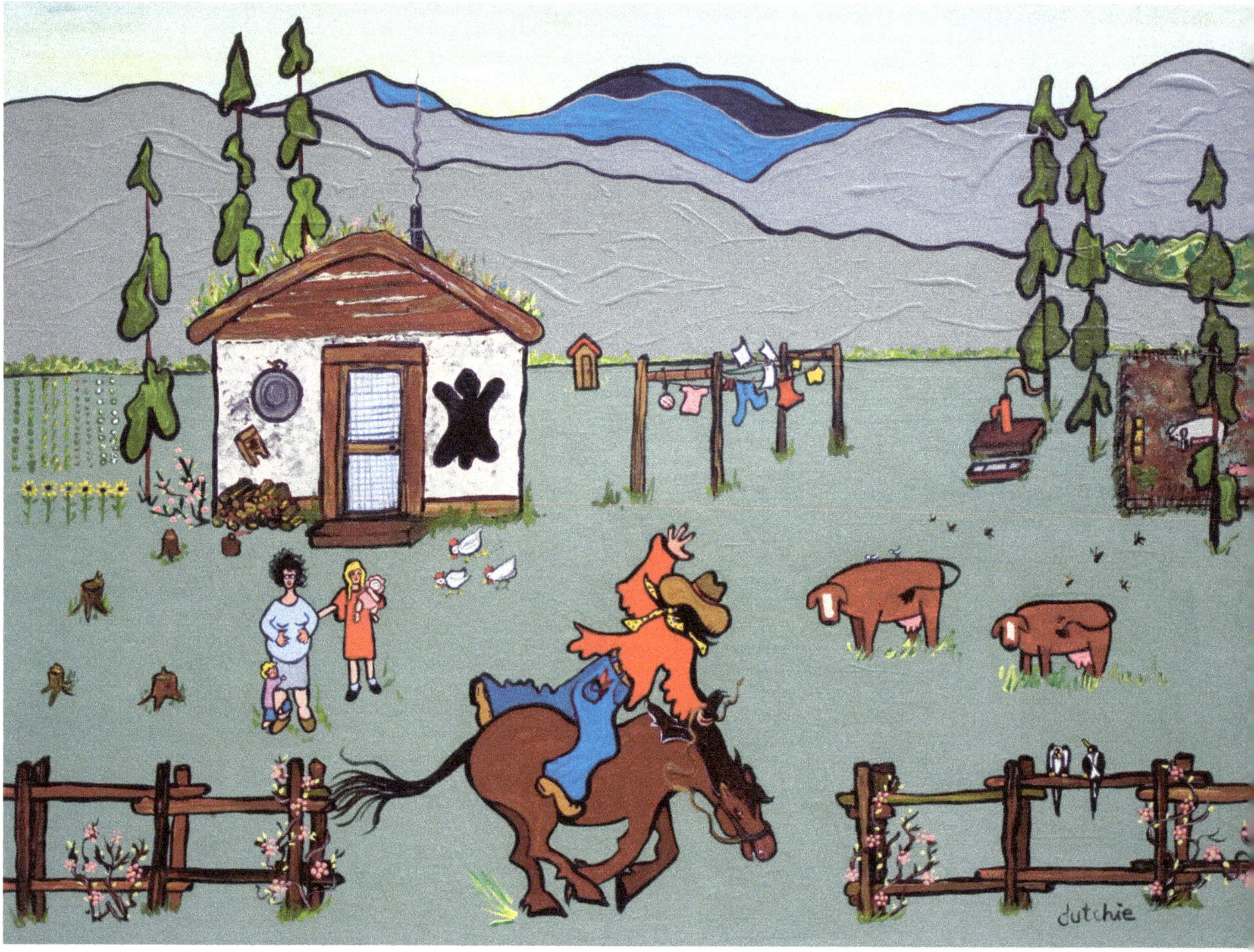

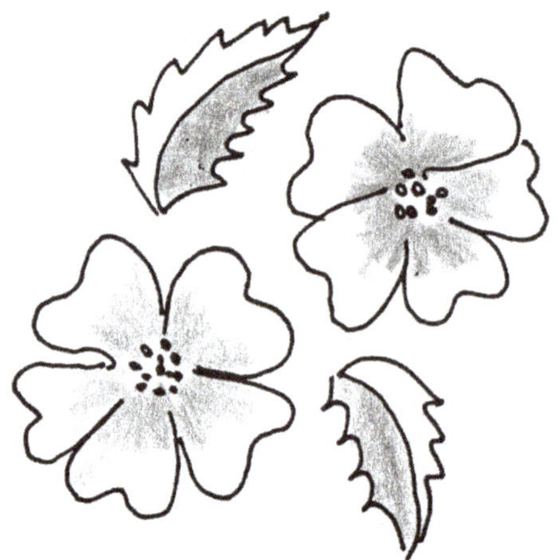

The Day the Twins Were Born
acrylic / canvas
66 x 51 cm

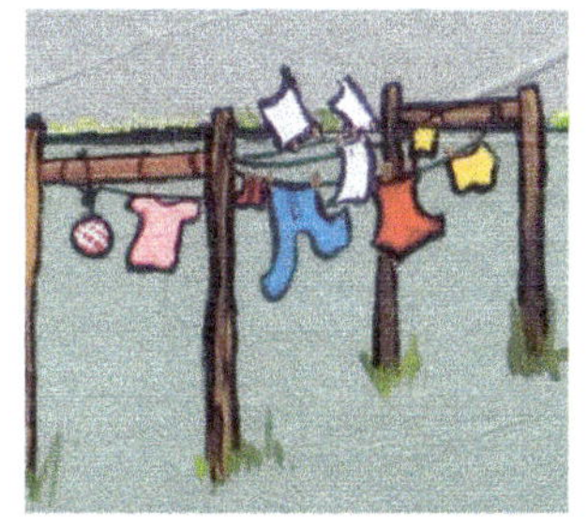

This is a book of memories — memories I have experienced or lived vicariously through the wonderful storytellers of the valley. Therefore, I think a good place to continue is the day I was born.

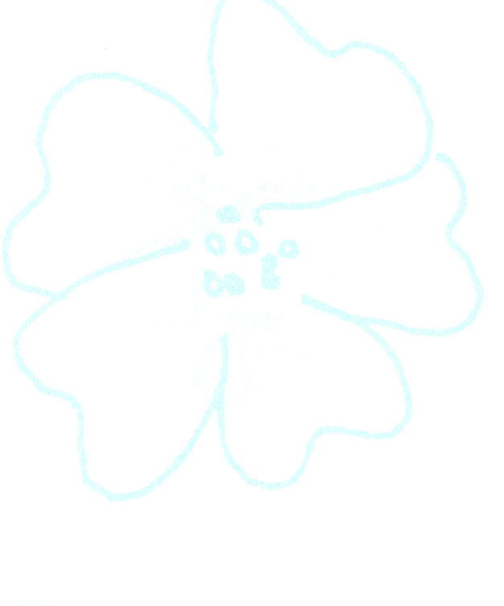

Mom told me that on the morning of August 9, 1938 she woke to the sound of wind. It carried to her the scent of the wild roses she loved. It was blistering hot and the wind was welcome. She was nine months pregnant, bigger than she had been with my sisters, by now 18 months and three years old. However, no matter how tired she felt, she was a homesteader's wife and there were children to feed and chores to do.

Early that August morning she felt the first pangs of labor and asked Frankie, the 16-year-old girl who had been staying with her to go to the fields and get Dad. My dad, a quick-tempered Irishman, roared up from the fields and grabbed the tamer of the two horses, endeavoring to head her in the direction of the nearest town and district nurse some seven miles away. The last my mother saw of him that day was on old Silver kicking up her heels while Dad cursed and hung on for dear life.

Hours before Dad returned — without nurse — Mom, with Frankie's help, had delivered a healthy set of twins. Two more girls. My mother, like most valley women, had not been attended to by a doctor for any of her pregnancies and was unaware that she was carrying twins until Frankie, holding the first baby said, "My God, Emmie, here comes another one!"

I was the first of those twins.

The 1950s came, and when Mom could afford the odd luxury she would buy herself a small jar of Avon's "To A Wild Rose" cream sachet. To me, that became my mom's perfume.

Now over half a century later, the scent of wild roses brings tears to my eyes as I recall Mom's love of that flower and the way she smelled when she hugged me.

3 Red Shoes

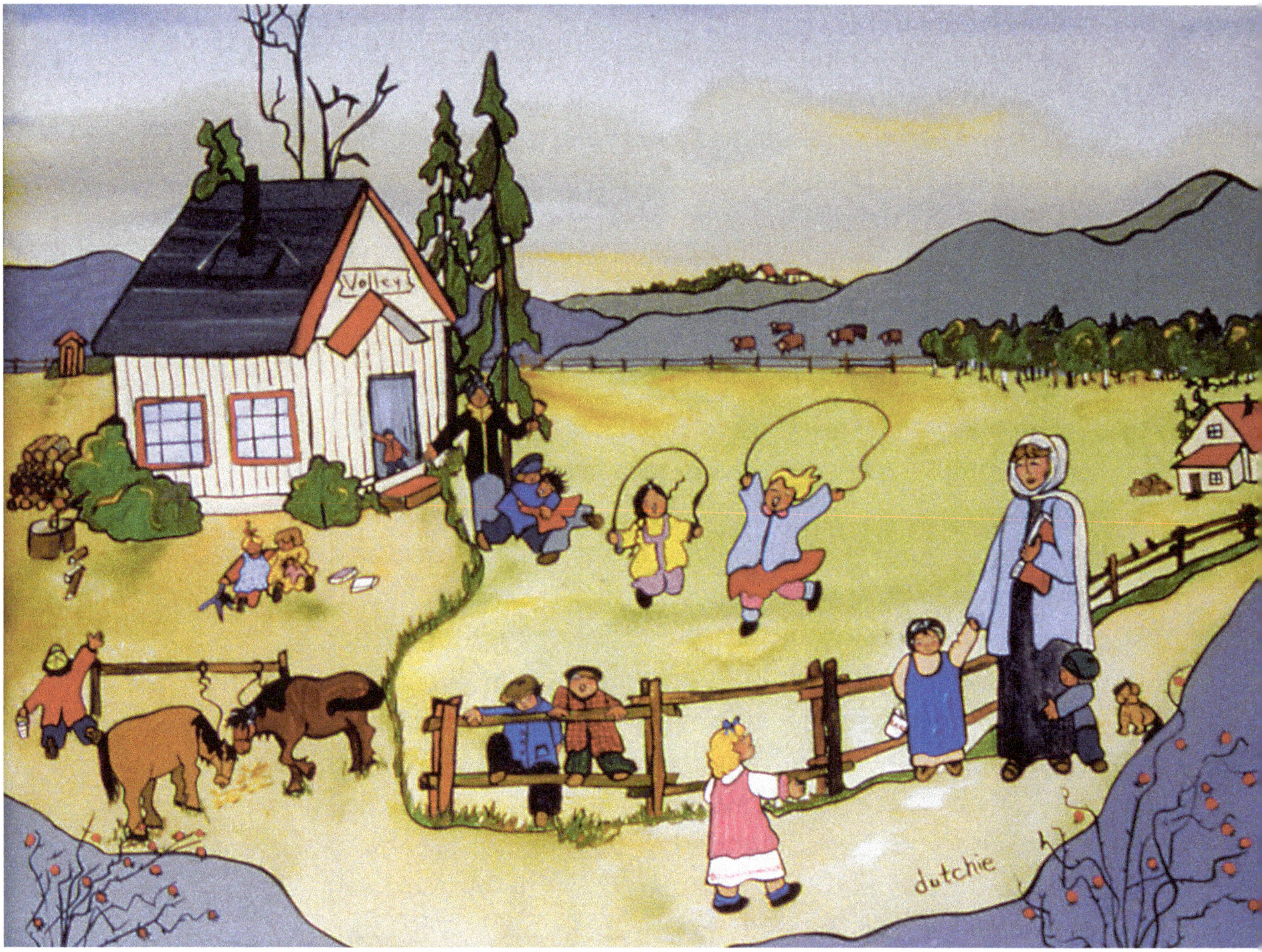

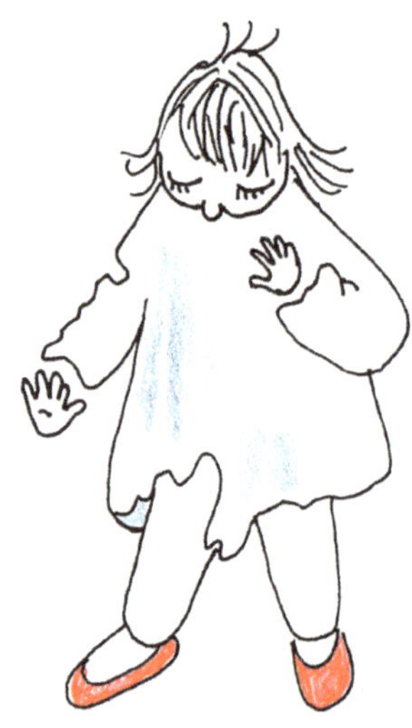

First Day of School
acrylic / canvas
51 x 66 cm
Collection: Kinusayo Museum

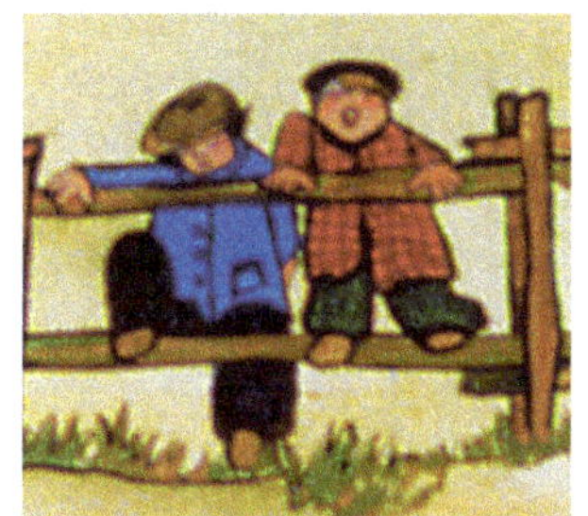

We lived seven miles from town. Because of this, my twin and I were deemed too small to hike the miles to school as required by our two older siblings. Therefore, Mom taught us at home until grade two; we were then considered big enough to walk three miles twice daily to catch a ride to the school.

We were country kids. The town children seemed confident and outgoing. They belonged and we didn't. Their clothes were store brought. Their lunches were made of thin slices of "store" bread.

How I envied their dainty shoes. Because of the distance we walked our footwear was practical, made to endure and keep the bitter cold from freezing our feet. I remember poring over the Eaton's catalogue for long hours, thinking if only I could have those red shoes I would be beautiful.

It didn't take long, though, for us to find our niche and we soon learned country kids were no less clever, and often more resourceful, than our town cousins.

4 Long Walk

I created *The Long Walk Home* because I remember it as a time of determined silence and ever changing color. The winter sun sank beneath the horizon well before we reached home and painted pictures on the drifting snow — yellows, pinks, and red, to midnight blue and the blackness of a starlit night. When the snow fell and the wind swept it across the land and buried the homestead fences, we nestled our faces into our scarves and watched our feet walk home.

On the coldest of nights the smoke from the chimney in our home would rise straight up into the sky. The light from the windows welcoming us was a comfort I shall never forget. I never understood until I was much older what Dad meant when he referred to the lighted windows as "the golden orbs of welcome". Now I know that beneath his farmer façade lurked the heart of a poet.

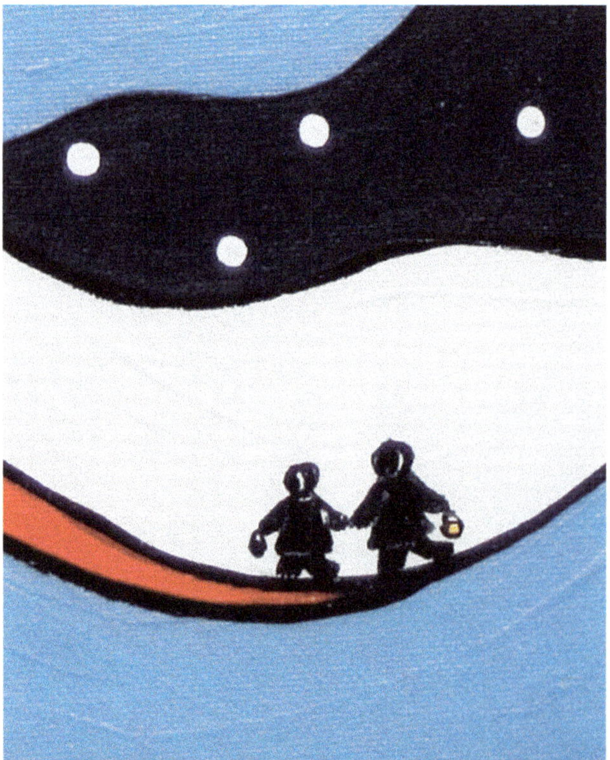

Long Walk Home
acrylic / canvas
44 x 60 cm

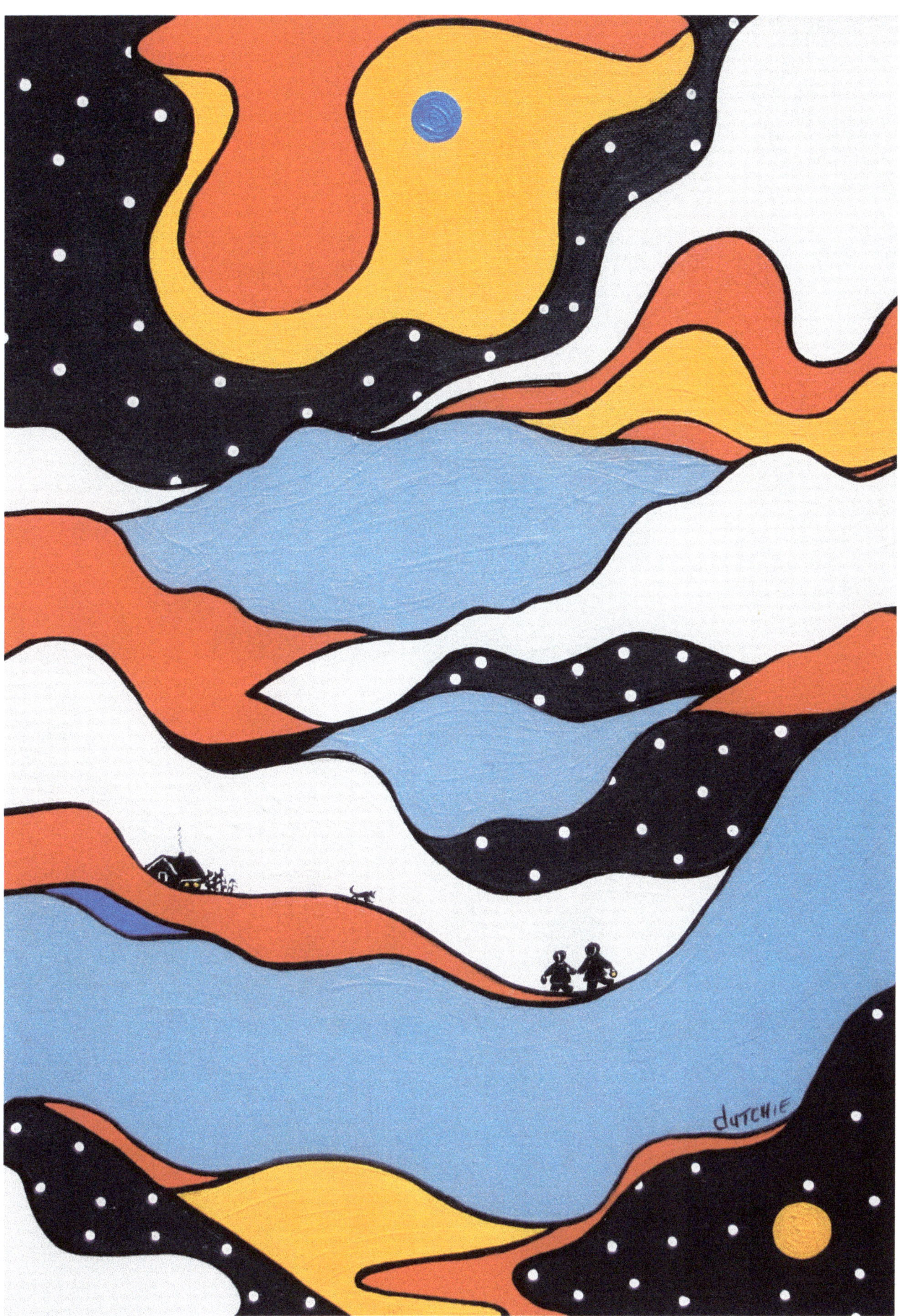
dutchie

5 Trap Line

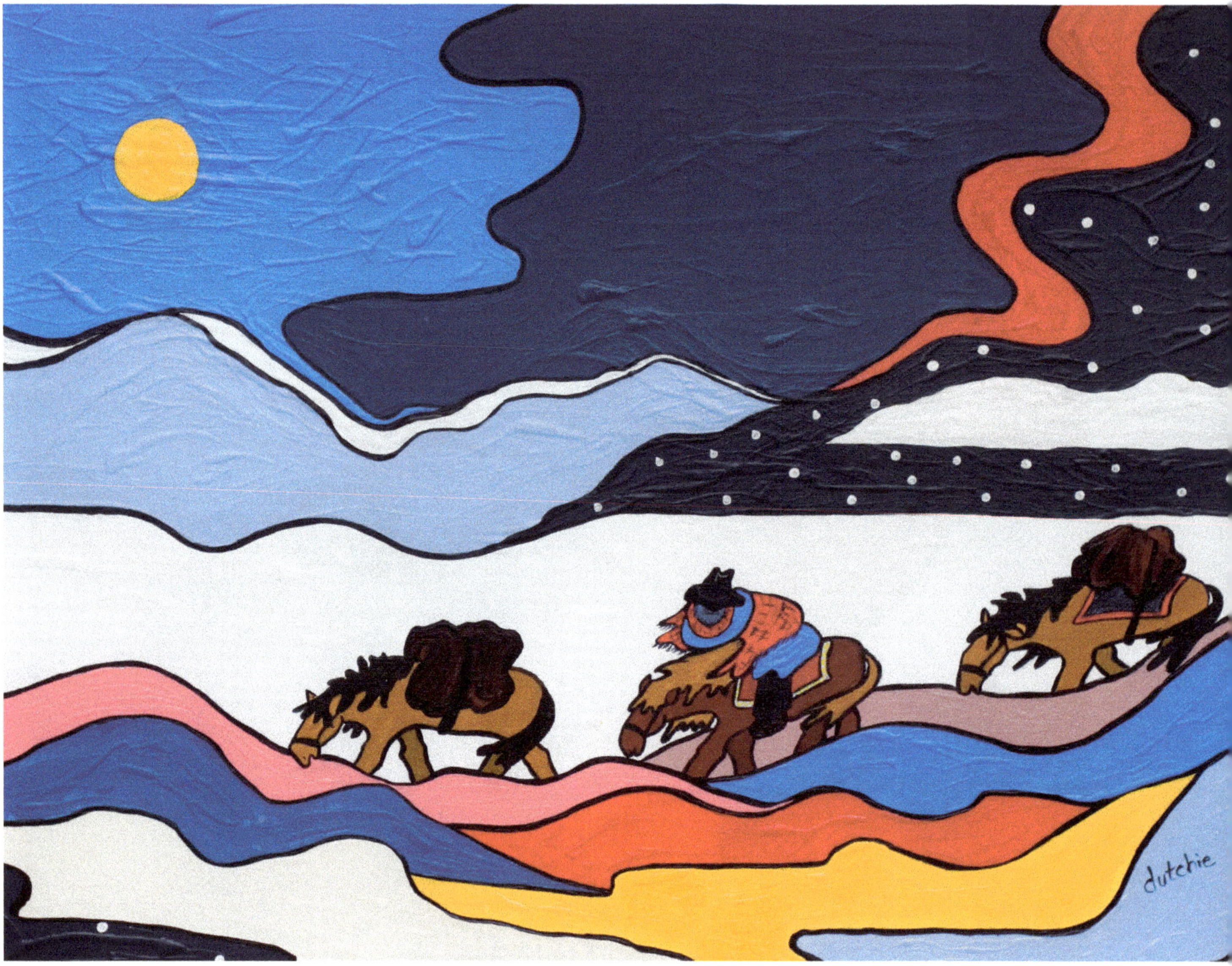

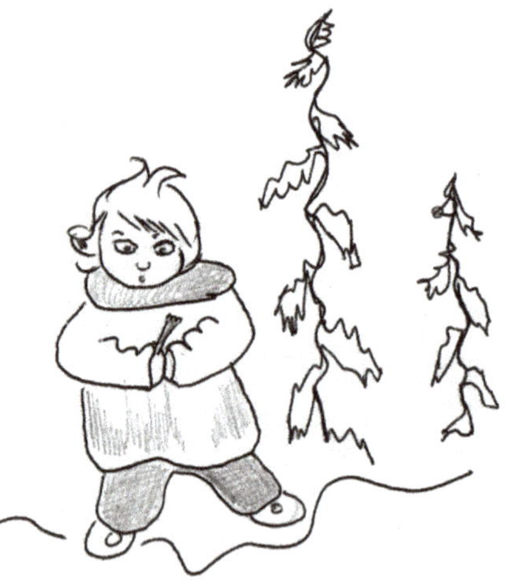

The Trapper
acrylic / canvas
51 x 66 cm

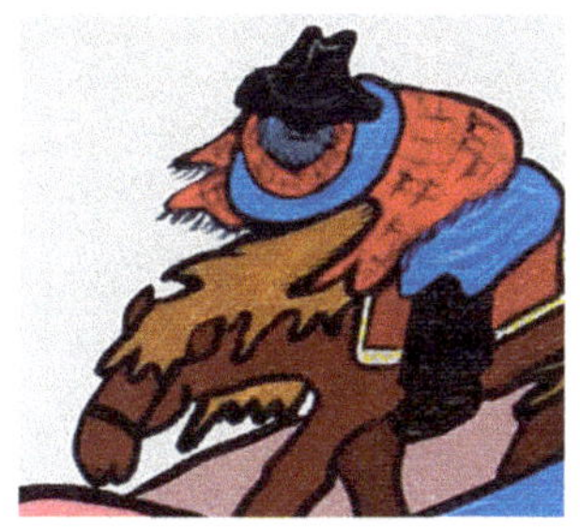

Several times a week my sister, Blackie, and I would check our trap line on the way home from school. I was reminded of this a few weeks back when my seven-year-old grandson, Danté, asked, "What did you do, Grandma, when you were a kid that you wished you had not done?"

I knew he must be guilty of something. But I didn't dwell on it because I was suddenly back a half century ago standing beneath the dense spruce that surrounded our farm taking careful aim at a small red squirrel.

I told Danté about the squirrels I used to shoot and catch in my leg hold traps and how I am still sorry that I killed all those little animals. He looked at me and I knew that he had just seen a side of me that he didn't understand or like very much. I tried to explain that it was our way of life; that I had shot prairie chickens for food and trapped weasels, mink, and squirrels for money. He could not understand how I could do such a cruel thing. We ended our conversation with him declaring. "Boy I could never do that," and me thinking, "Why the hell didn't I just lie?"

Our conversation ended but my thoughts carried on. My sister and I, like most farm kids in the area, had an unregistered trap line, which meant that we staked out an area around our homestead and set traps. It was considered less than honorable to rob anyone else's traps; however, if I recall correctly, our trap line honor slipped once or twice. We learned how to bait traps and to remove small frozen bodies from their cruel leg holds without damaging the fur. We took our catch home, thawed it out by the wood stove, then skinned and stretched our pelts.

The time I remember with the most remorse is when, upon checking a trap, I found only a small weasel leg, chewed off by its owner, at the edge of steel that had held him prisoner.

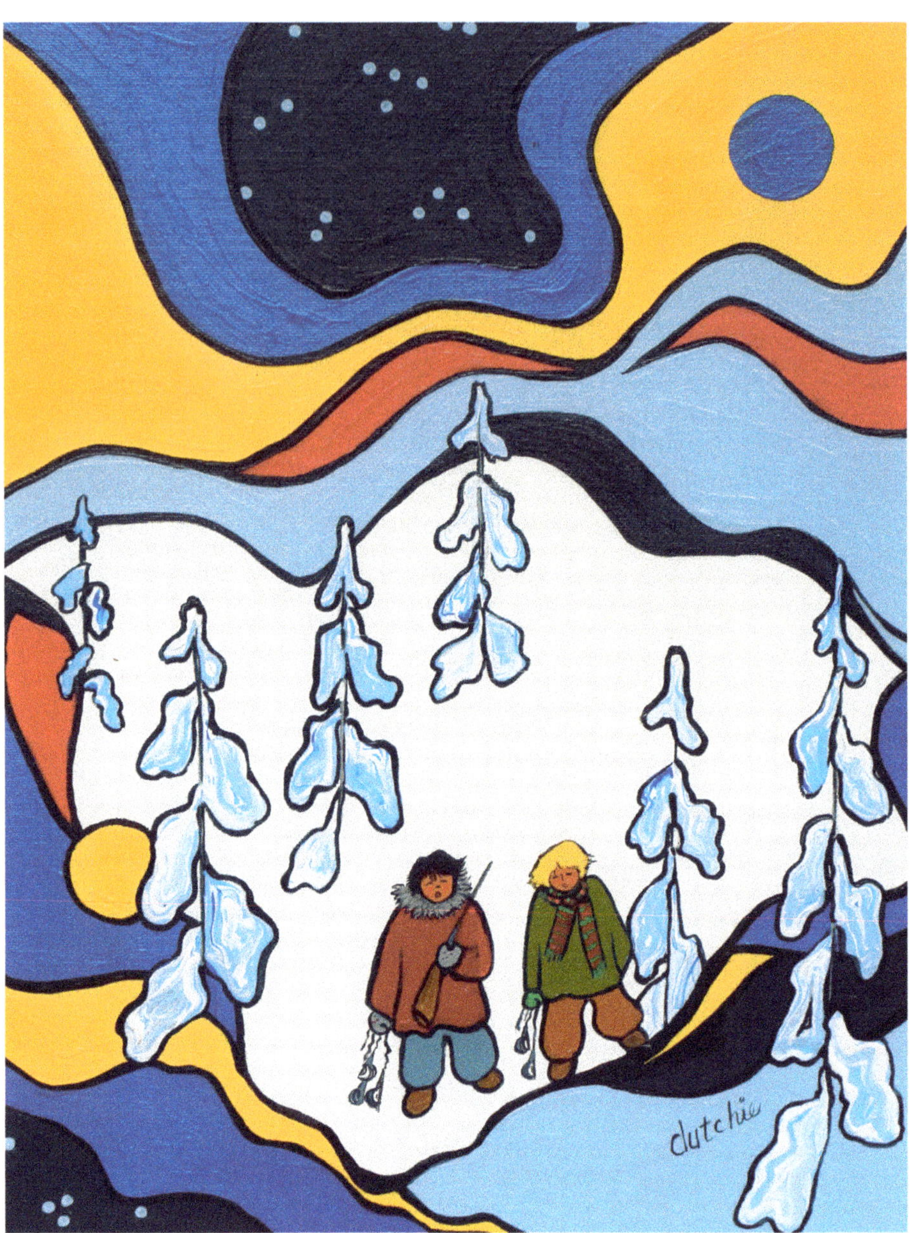

The Trap Line
acrylic / canvas
34 x 44 cm

I know times are different now. We were survivors; we all did what we had to do. But I still wish I could give life back to all those little animals whose coats I sold for thirty-five cents.

When Danté is older I will try again to tell him about my "trapping youth". Perhaps he will judge me less harshly. I hope so.

Lesson 6

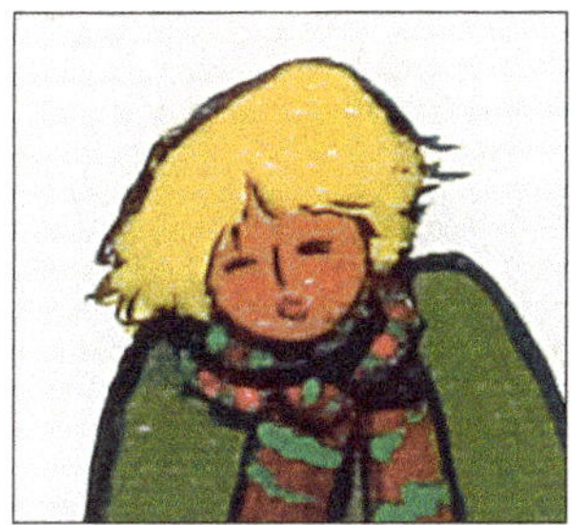

Years later I returned to the North as a first-year teacher in Dawson Creek, a BC farming community. My class was a group of teenagers who, according to those who "knew best," did not belong in a regular classroom, whatever that meant. In reality what it did mean was that a group of Native and farm kids who were tired of being let down by the educational system were lumped together in one room and labeled "special needs."

They were ready for me when I stepped into the classroom. They were defiant and, frankly, quite tired of their status in the school. To them there was only one person lower on the totem pole than they were...me. Indeed they were special — especially angry — and I was their target. To make matters worse I did not know what the hell I was doing. We were a combination of human personalities ready to explode, and I had little doubt that they would not be the losers.

What I did know were animals. Being a farm kid I had learned that animals respond to kindness a whole lot better than to being bullied into behaving. I don't think it was a conscious decision, but because I didn't know what else to do I tried gentle persuasion. I told them how glad I was to be in Dawson Creek and how lucky I was to have them for my very first class. I then confessed that I did not know what to do and that they would have to help me.

Northern folks are reared helping each other; it's a wonderful part of their culture. You never leave friend or

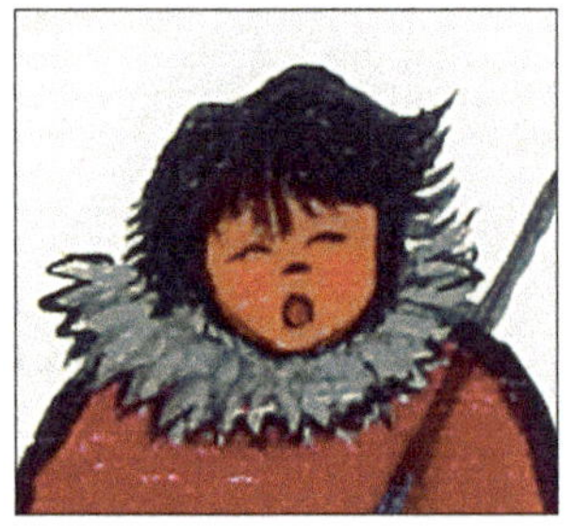

stranger in a snowy ditch, or in a classroom. Because of this they were ready to help me. They loved the fact I had admitted that I did not know what to do, and before the week was up my kids and I had an unspoken pact. As long as we were happy and learning, it was no one else's business how we tackled the job. We learned together, my kids and I. The administration and the rest of the staff who taught "regular" students were none the wiser. We were happy finding our own way.

Every one of my kids was at a different level. A fifteen year old could only read at a grade two level, while another could sketch a winter scene that would bring tears to your eyes but did not know the multiplication tables. One thing they all had in common: they were survivors.

I soon discovered that just about everything I had learned at university was useless in the North; instead of getting the kids to adapt to my way of thinking I had to, for survival purposes, find out in a real hurry how to communicate with them. And I did! I particularly remember two occasions.

The first was a challenge by a young man who declared loudly that I could hardly know what it was like to be a northern kid when I came from Vancouver. I told him that I was raised on a farm and that I used to trap and shoot squirrels and weasels and sell their furs. He plainly did not believe me. He sneered as I pushed my case further and told the class that I had regularly skinned squirrels as a youngster. This was met with giggles of disbelief. I was trapped. What to do to gain back their respect? Being a survivor myself and not one to rely too heavily on book learning as the only educational tool, I picked up a piece of chalk and drew a two-foot picture of a dead squirrel stretched out on his back on the chalk board. Using chalk like I would a skinning knife I said, "The first thing you do is cut around their little asshole,

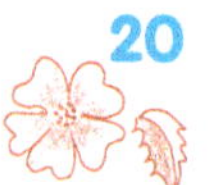

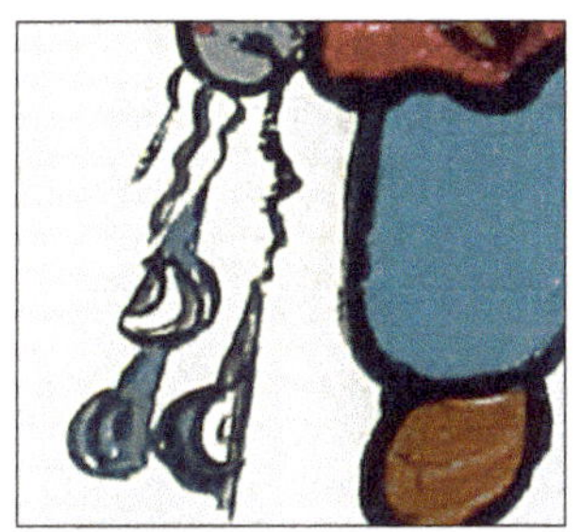

then make a sharp cut down the inside of each leg before you cut off their hind feet. Be very careful you do not cut off the tail as a tailless squirrel is worth much less than one with tail attached." They were delighted. They never questioned my language, after all that is how they skinned their squirrels. I belonged.

The second occasion I recall was during a reading lesson. I just could not get most of the kids to understand that they could tackle a word phonetically; "sounding out" a word just never made sense. I think God was in my classroom that day because suddenly I knew how to get them to understand the elusive concept of breaking a word down to its parts. Again I picked up a piece of chalk and printed in large bold letters the word "SHIT". I asked if someone would read the word out loud for me. They yelled in unison SHIT! "Great," I said, "now let's look at this word," and printed SH…IT. Total silence and bigger smiles. For the rest of the year whenever I heard "sh...it" whispered softly I knew some kid was tackling a new word.

That year I was to realize many times that lessons I had learned as a northern farm kid were more valuable to my class and me than all the "book learnin'" I had done at university. Indeed, my kids were "special."

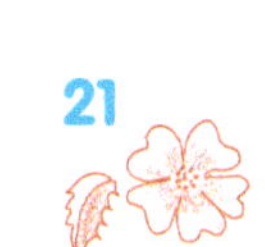

7 Chores

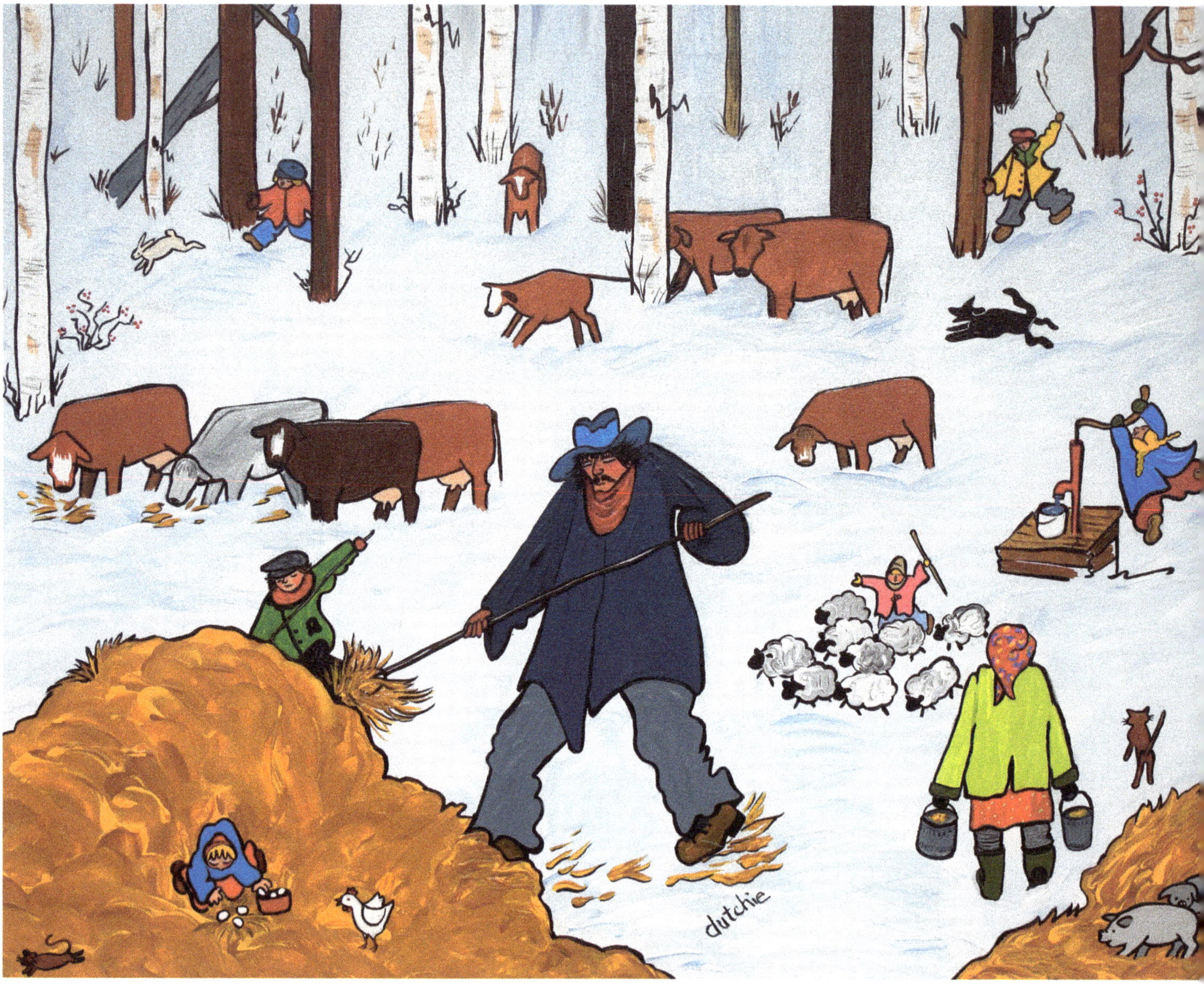

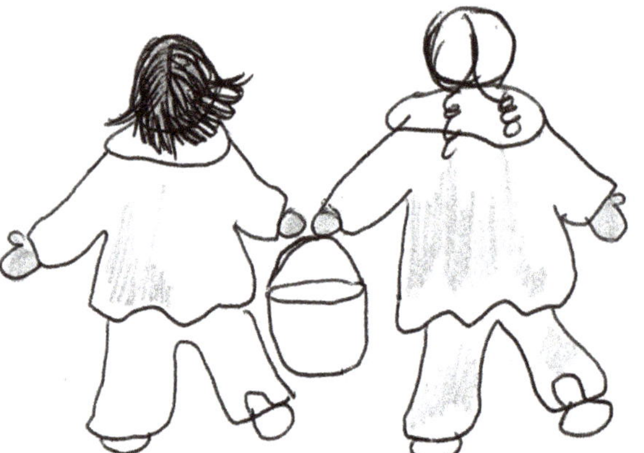

Morning Chores
acrylic / canvas
61 x 77 cm

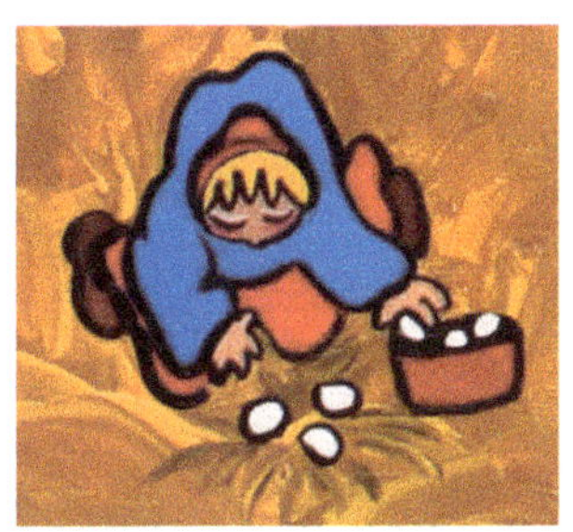

We learned at an early age that everyone was expected to contribute to the labor required to clothe and feed a family of eight. There were cows to herd, cows to feed, cows to milk; barns to clean; pigs to swill, and eggs to gather; water to pump and buckets of water to be toted across the yard to fill the ice well so that we would have cold storage for the hot Alberta summers; sheep to gather, sheep to count to make sure that none had fallen victim to hungry, lurking coyotes; wood to chop and wood boxes to fill...and, finally, breakfast.

No one ever said they were not hungry.

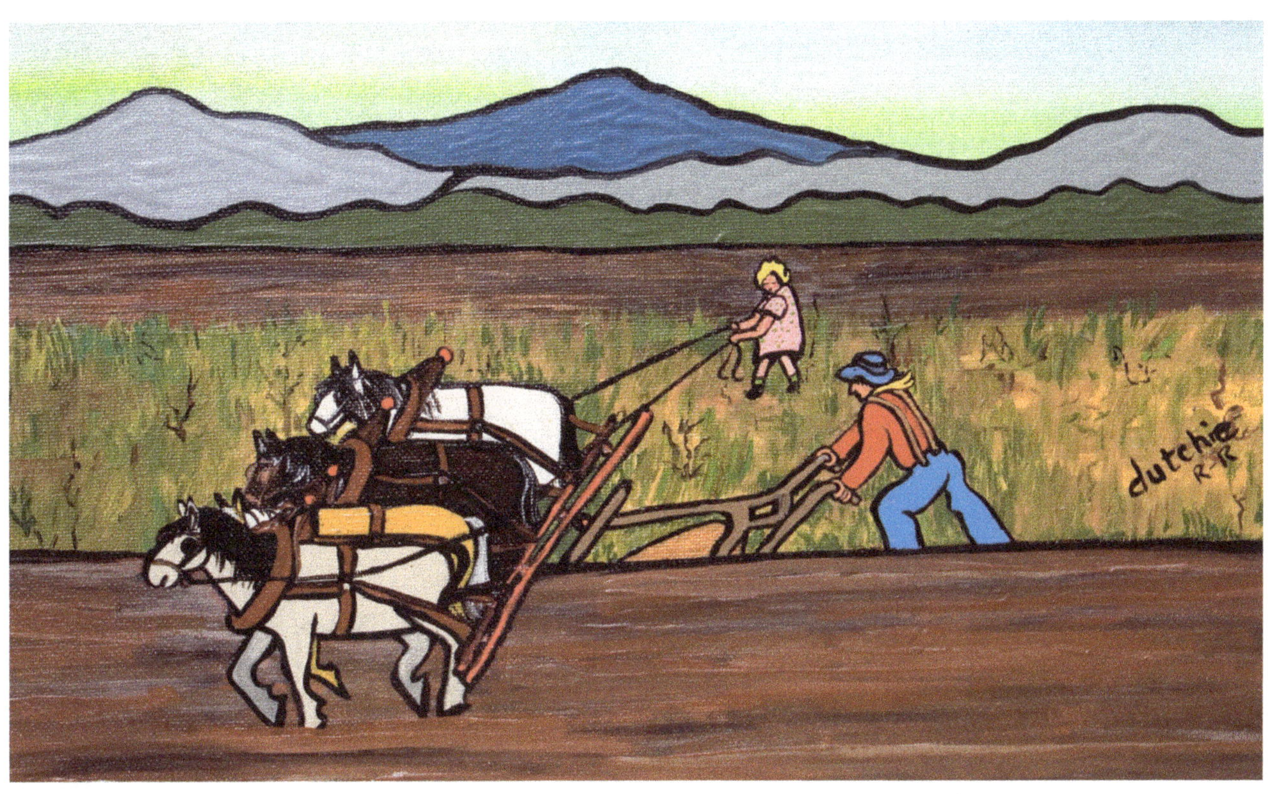

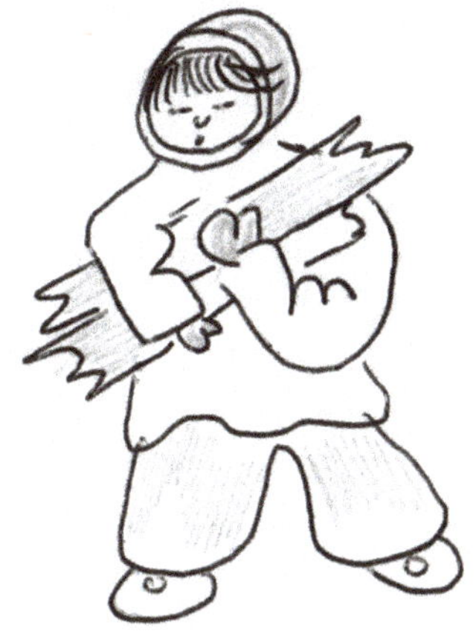

My Sister Arlene

acrylic / canvas

44 x 23 cm

Collection: Arlene Rutledge-Reed

8 Stampede

The last days of school meant the coming of a long, hot summer filled with the necessary work to feed and shelter our family for the next onslaught of winter. Our childhood thoughts, however, were not on the summer's toil but on the upcoming festivities. Dominion Day meant three days of celebration and was a much-anticipated event. I remember well the excitement. The music. The colors. The food. A time when cultural differences were put aside and we celebrated as one.

There were dances, baseball games, races, and many other activities for both kids and adults. The stampede, however, is the event that I remember most clearly. Faithful horses that had pulled plows in springtime were pushed into service as "bucking broncos." Ewes that had labored with lambs just short months earlier were herded into the corral where young lads would enter the ring and pretend they were Hopalong Cassidy, Tom Mix, Roy Rogers, or other frontier heroes. Steers were reluctantly prodded into the arena; farmhands crawled onto their backs and hoped the animals had enough spirit to buck. We hollered and cheered like they were riding the world's meanest critters.

The Native folks set up their tents in the forest

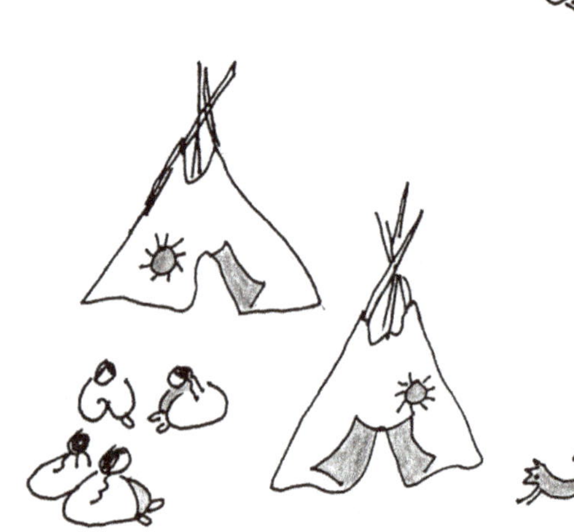

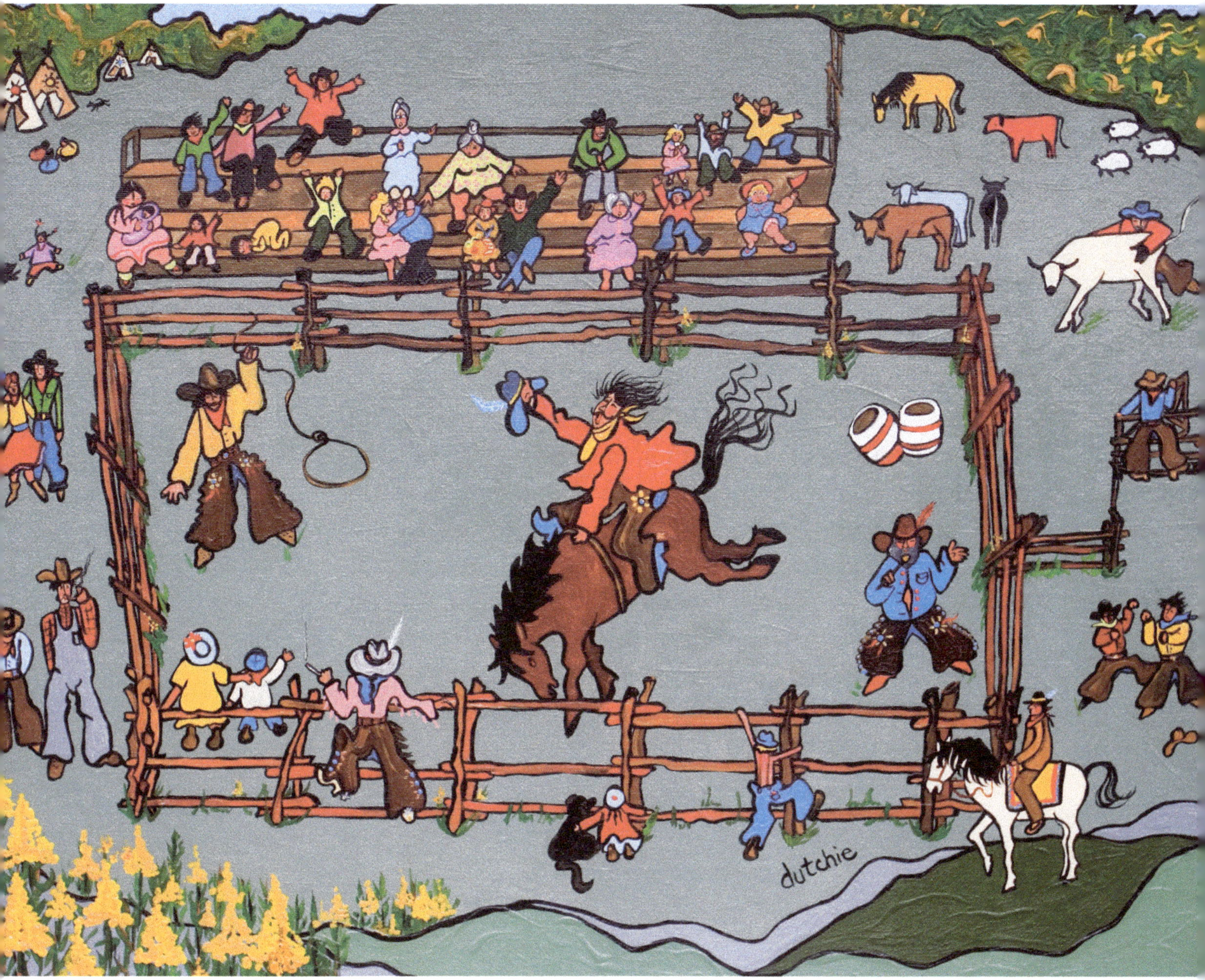

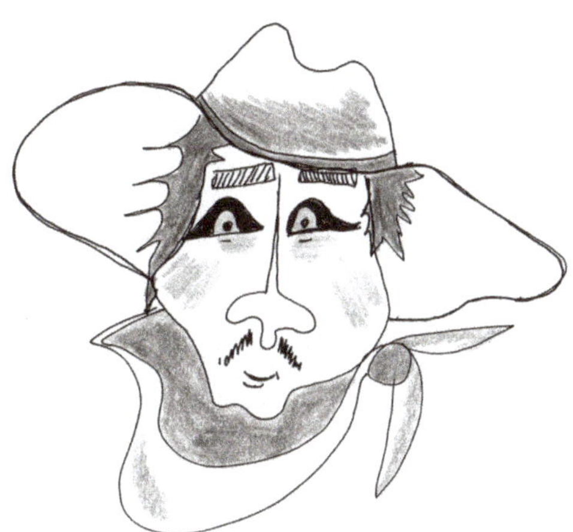

Stampede . . . the Dude

acrylic / canvas

51 x 66 cm

Collection: Alberta Department of Northern Affairs

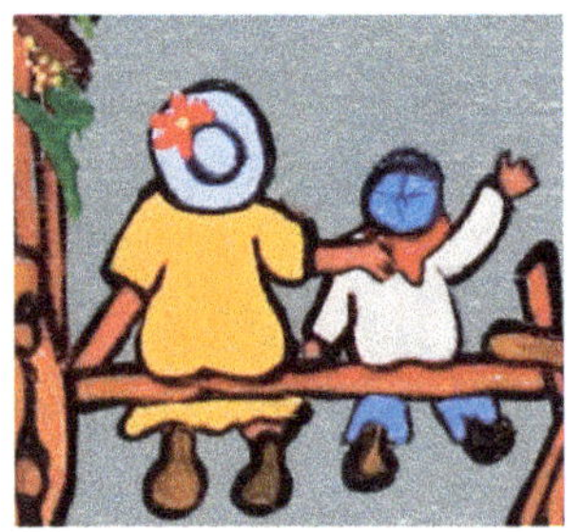

behind the stockyards. Their young men sat tall and proud on prancing ponies. Farm lads looked on with envy knowing that their only steed had to be a large, sturdy "all purpose vehicle."

The painting *Stampede…The Dude*, so named after a dear old cowboy with whom we have celebrated many a Calgary Stampede, gave me much pleasure as memories poured forth through my fingers. I felt like a child once more. I used a magnifying glass to paint each tiny face. As I painted, I recalled the folks I cared about and those who were a general pain in the butt — like the lady tapping the young couple on the shoulder. Anything fun was immoral to her and she was the first to fink to our parents at the least infraction. And so my characters went as true to life as I recall. I wanted to give my viewers a moment of history where hard work was the norm but joyous hearts prevailed. I hope I have done that for you. "The Dude" is the gentleman with the mike. May he forgive me the tummy.

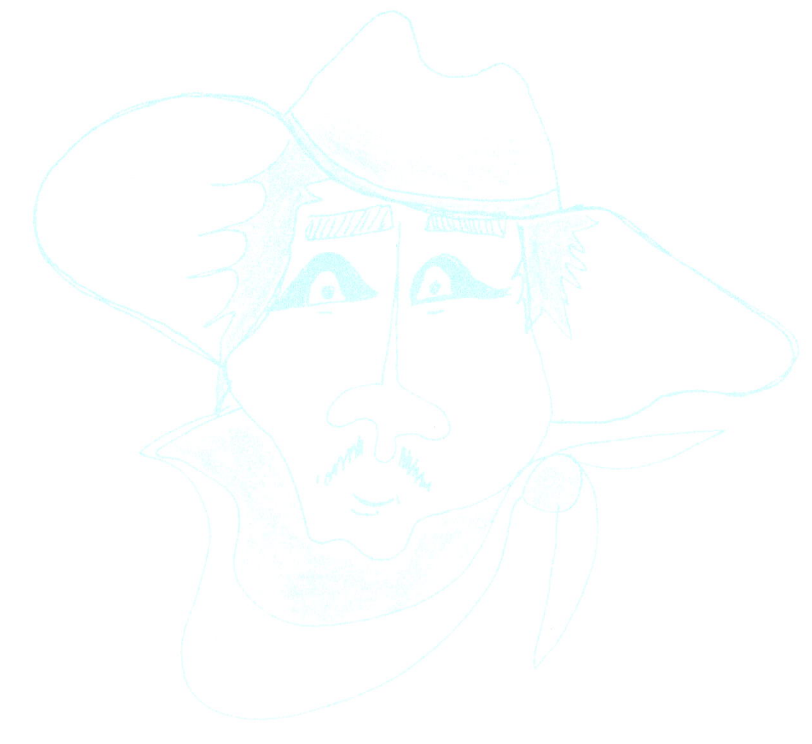

Potato 9

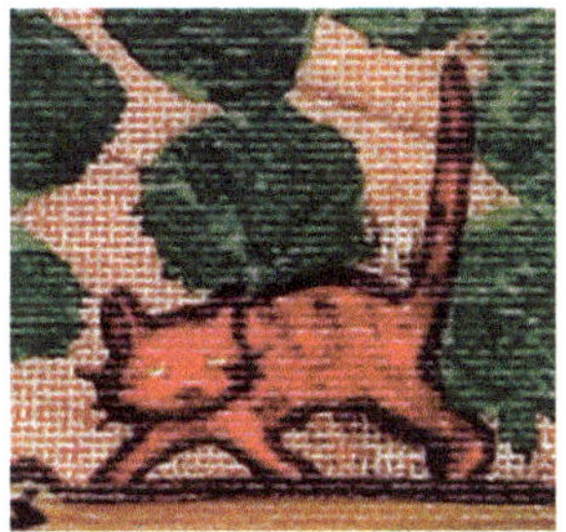

The three days of celebration ended. Cows became just that again, and the bucking broncos were once again hooked to the plow. The farm kids returned to homesteads. The summer's work began. It was endless.

A large garden was not only a source of pride but also a necessity, as it had to provide enough root vegetables to feed a family of eight during the lengthy northern winters.

The potato patch. I don't know how to tell you how damned big the thing was. Let me digress. I married a young airman in 1955. Five days later he was posted with NATO in England. Two months later I followed. We spent over three wonderful years there and I, who had never been far south of Edmonton, was in awe of everything. Paved roads. Electricity. Indoor plumbing. The crowds. People everywhere. However, I continually told Tom about this beautiful home in my village, owned by a local merchant, and how my dream was to have a home equally fine someday.

On being posted back to Canada I proudly took him home to view my childhood mansion. We drove around the block several times before I was forced to admit that the drab, little bungalow with the peeling, yellow paint was the golden castle of my youth. My disappointment was keen.

This is my roundabout way of telling you about the potato patch of my childhood. It did not look near as menacing when I returned thirty years later.

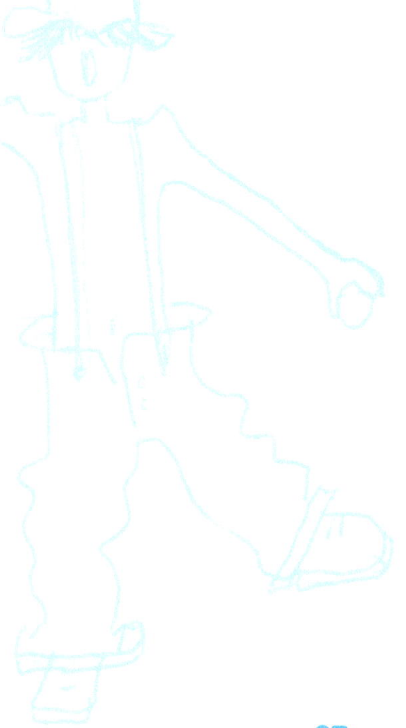

We not only grew potatoes for our own consumption, we also supplied local lumber mills. A bushel of new potatoes put one dollar into the family coffers.

The potato patch also offered fun times. After the harvest the potatoes deemed too small to use were left lying on the ground. There they froze solid by night only to melt in the midday sun. A thawed spud makes a wonderful squirt gun as it spews forth its liquid contents at the nearest victim. These wee potatoes caused many sibling spats as we chased each other around the plot. A mouth shot was considered a ten.

The Potato Patch caused much controversy among the valley men when I hung it with the *Homestead* collection. Apparently I was not the only "kid" who recalled hoeing endless rows of spuds under a searing summer sun.

It tickled me considerably when the old valley farmers gathered around the picture and argued who had had the largest potato patch. There did not seem to be a clear winner, as every "young heart" knew for darn sure that theirs was the biggest. I was told with great certainty that the Rutledge potato patch was no match for the spreading acres of a Sloan or Hunt crop. We argued happily back and forth, and all left knowing that ours was the largest and that the aging memories of others made their own potato patches bigger.

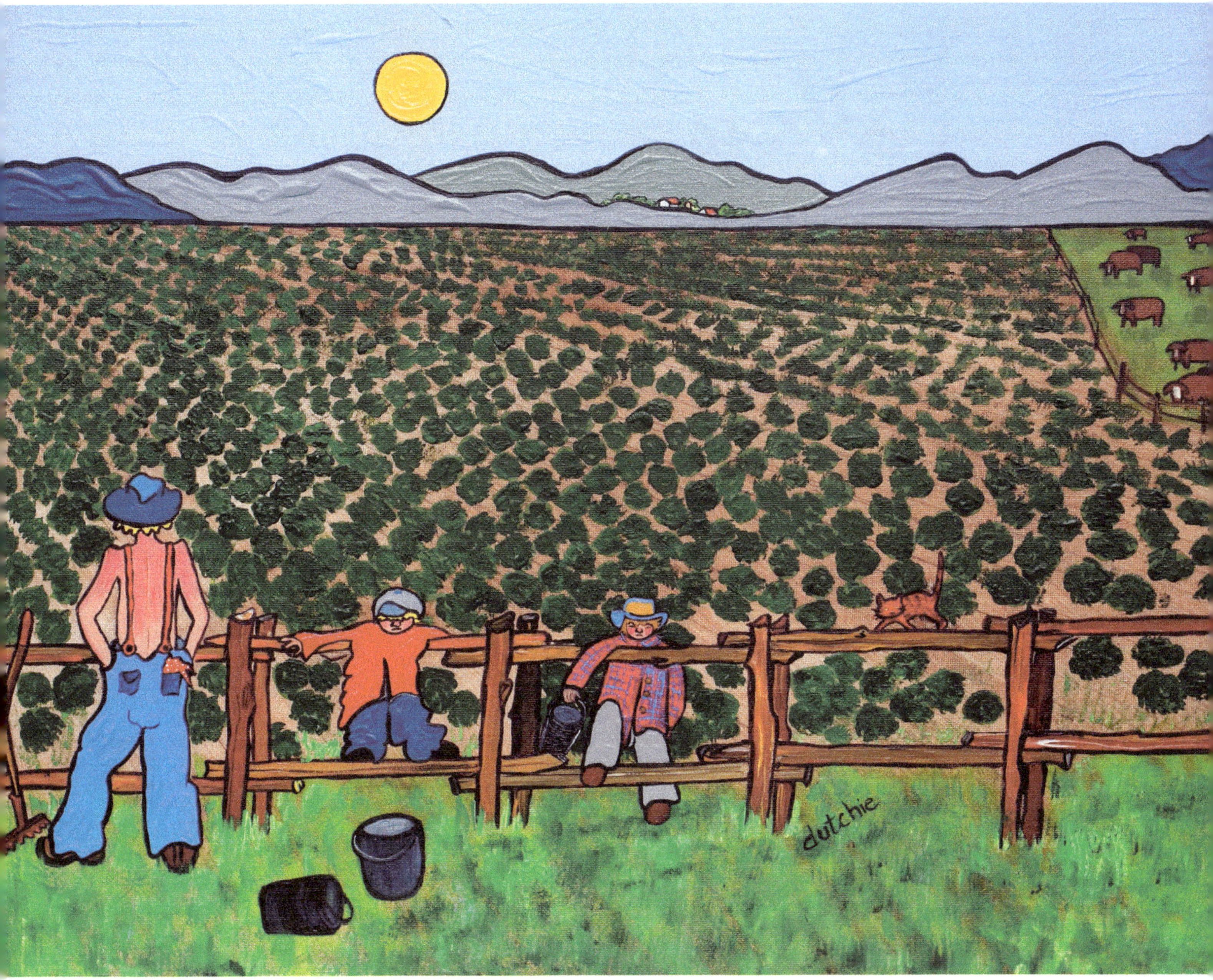

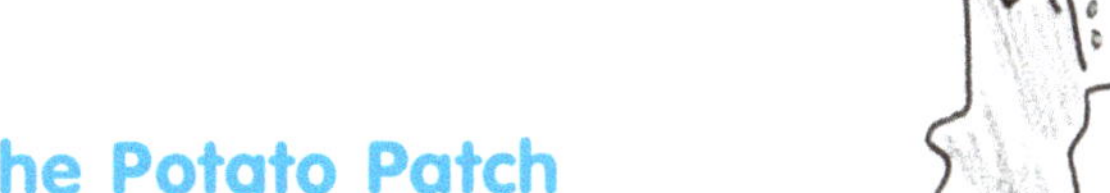

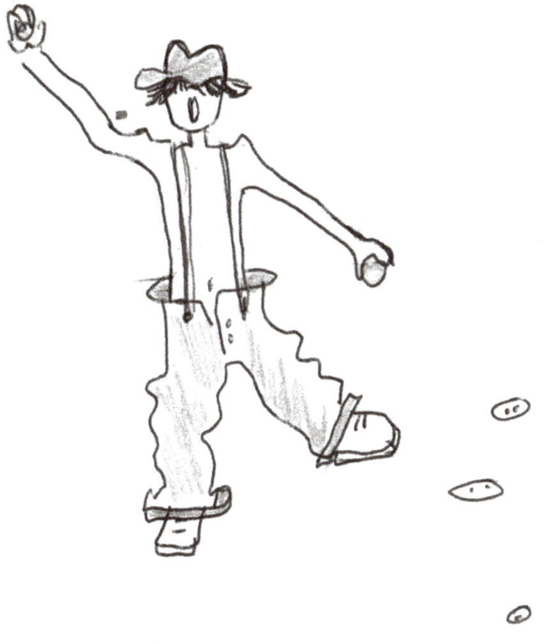

The Potato Patch
acrylic / canvas
51 x 66 cm

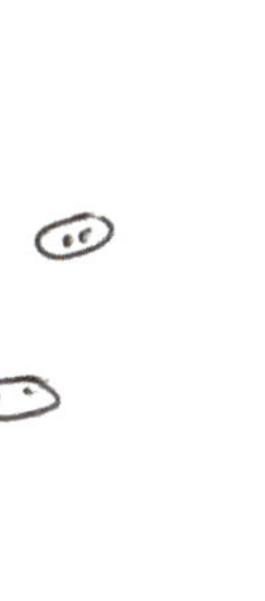

10 Hay

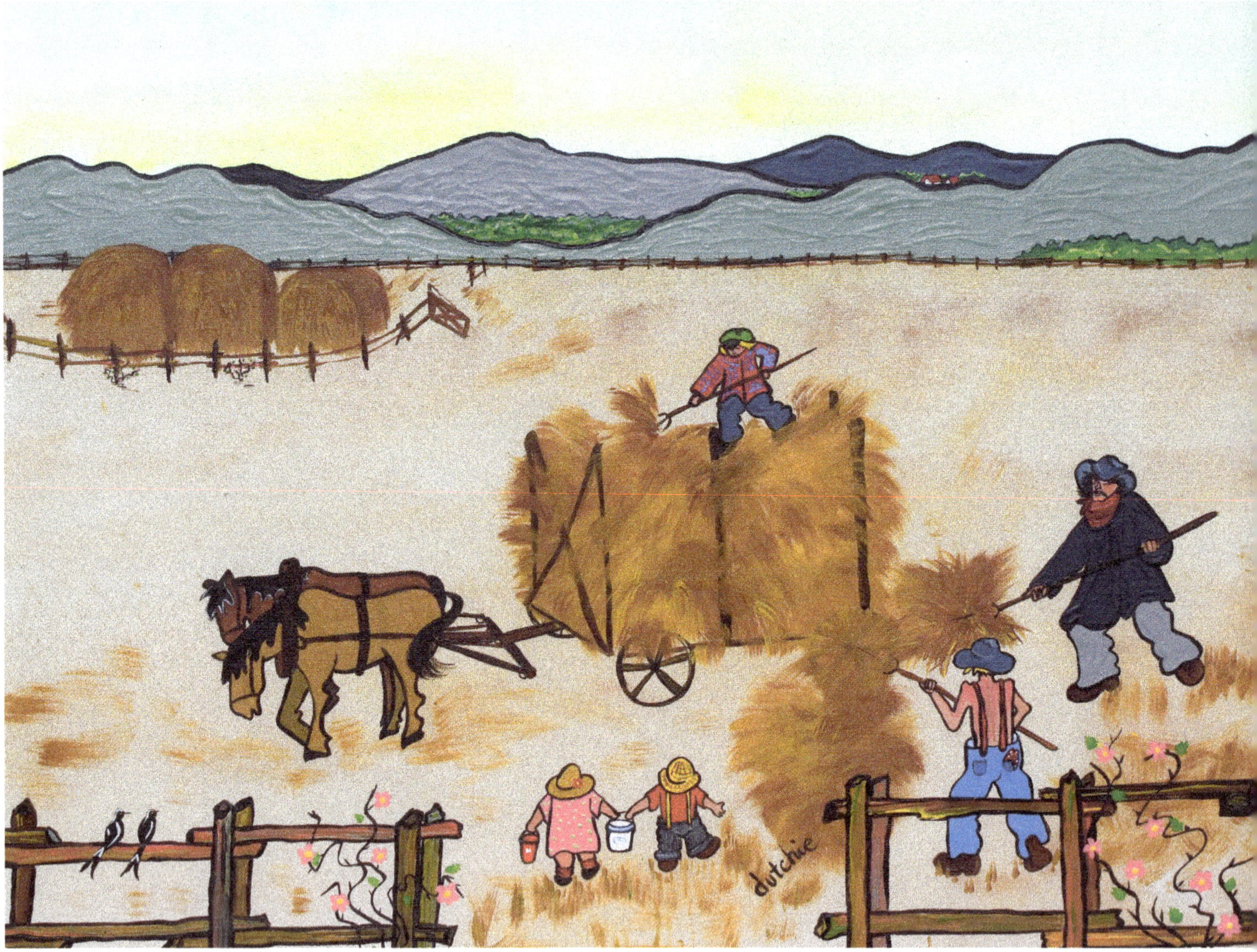

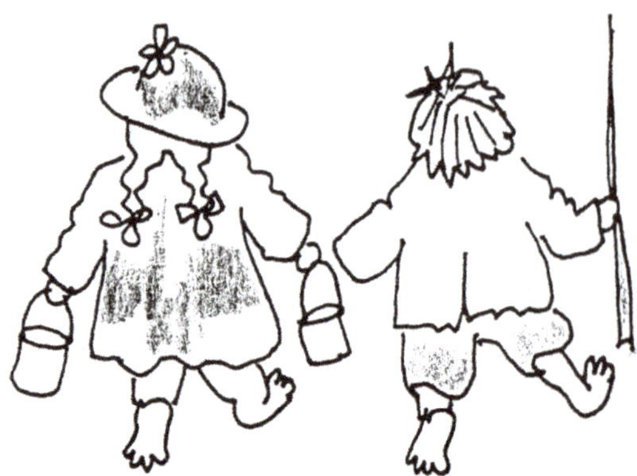

Haying Time
acrylic / canvas
51 x 66 cm

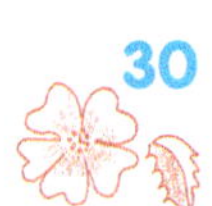

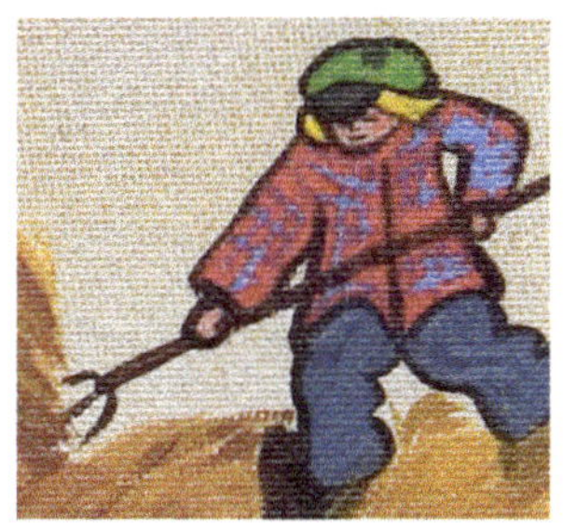

The wonderful scent of fresh-cut hay lingers, I am sure, in the hearts of all farm kids. Prior to the 1950s this wondrous smell came at the price of hours of hard labor beneath an unforgiving sun. It was always a race. Get that hay cut. Get it raked. Dry it. Gather it. Hurry! Hurry! Stack it before the next sudden thunderstorm.

This surge of energy was vital. If it rained, the hay had to be turned several times to make sure that it was thoroughly dry before it could be stacked. Mildewed hay could not be fed to stock. It's a backbreaking job turning fifty acres of hay by hand with a pitchfork. And who knew when it might rain again.

The need for speed required that all family members help with the job. The youngest had the job of delivering lunch to the field. Never have fresh-cut onions between thick slices of homemade bread tasted so good. I remember well the welcome sight of two little figures carrying lard pails full of sandwiches to thirsty, hungry haymakers.

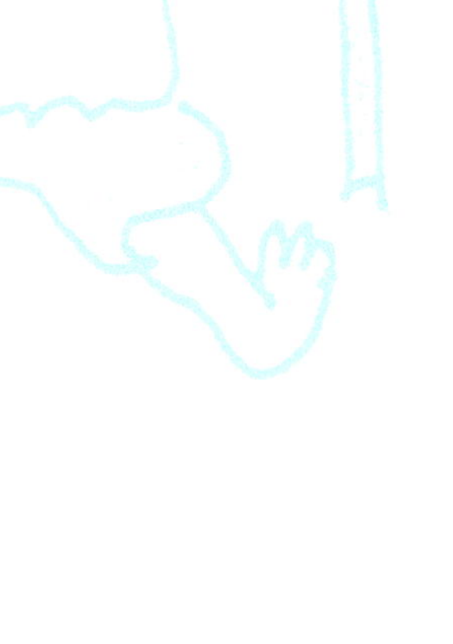

11 Sheep

We were subsistence homesteaders and everything we grew or raised ended up in the stew pot, or was sold for those necessities we could not grow or make. Hence, we had cattle, sheep, chickens, pigs, and horses. All this livestock required a certain amount of care, none more than the sheep.

At birthing time the ewes were in continual need of assistance, with a new mother often dying. Every spring we would have several lambs harbored safely behind Mom's wood stove in the kitchen. They were loved, cuddled, and bottle-fed until they were old enough to join the herd. By the time they hit the frying pan we had forgotten that we had raised them like babies.

Sheep required special fences as they were scroungers and could go under the average stock fence. Coyotes were their worst enemy. We tried home remedies to keep the coyotes at bay. I recall placing mothballs every few feet along the perimeter of the sheep yards. Lore held that coyotes would not come near because of the scent. Not true. It always came down to one of the kids to tend the sheep and keep an eye out for predators.

This was a coveted job as it got the lucky shepherd away from other farm chores. A time to catch a snooze or read a book. Lady Luck looked after the sheep.

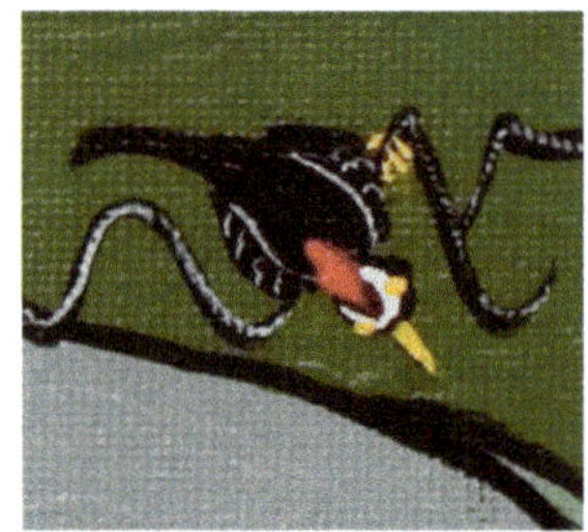

Tending The Sheep
acrylic / canvas
50 x 32 cm

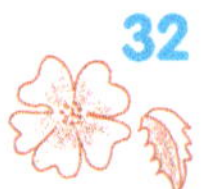

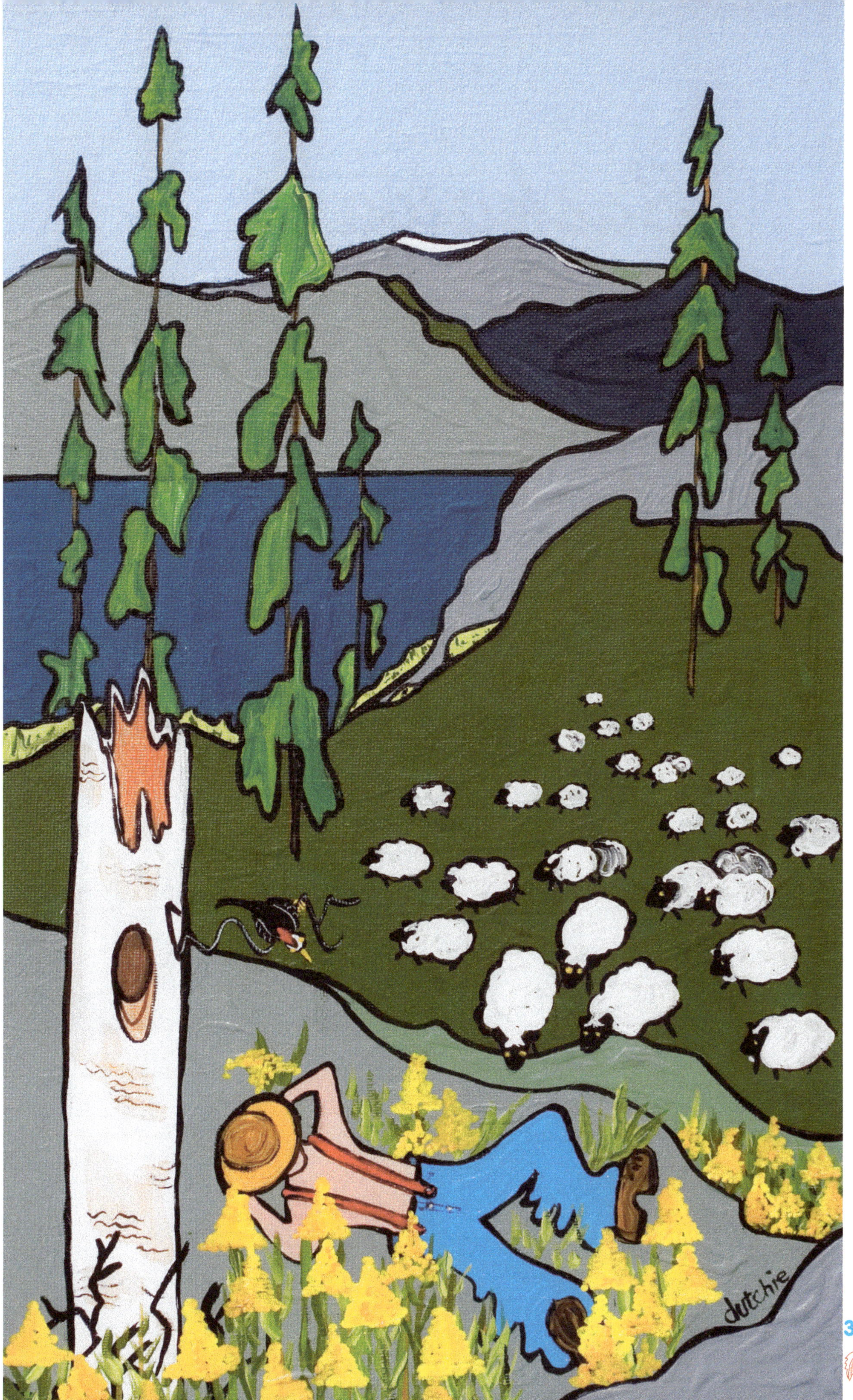
dutchie

12 Saskatoons

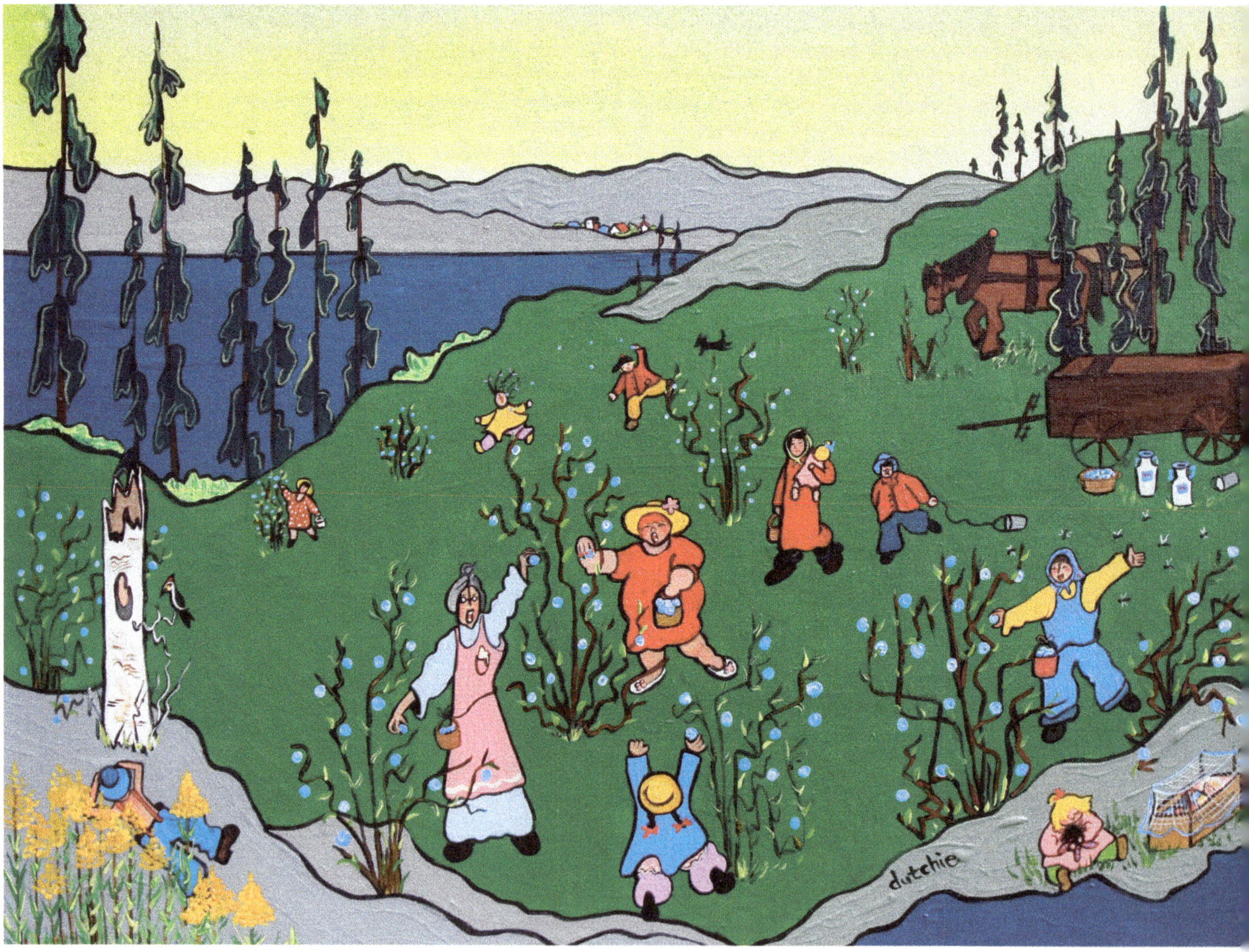

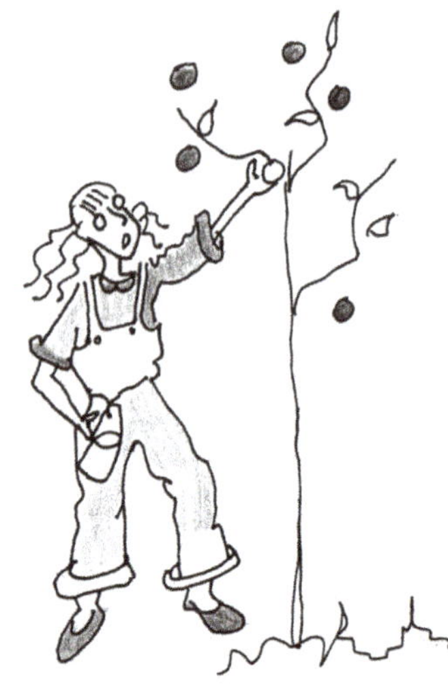

Saskatoon Patch
acrylic / canvas
66 x 51 cm

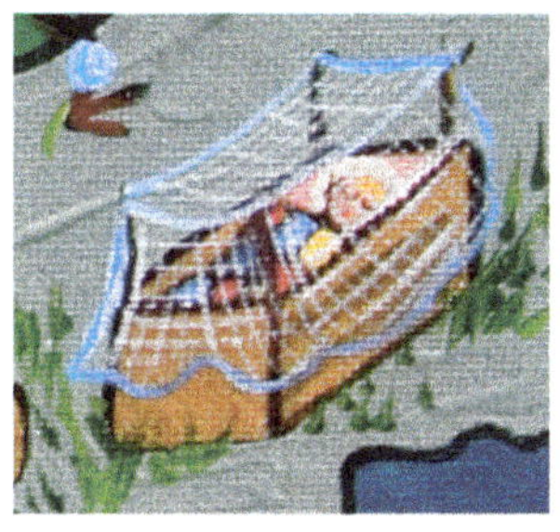

Our short northern summer ended and we were into harvest time. How well I remember this time of the year, not so much because it meant the end of summer's labor, but because every fall one large wooden box of Macintosh apples was purchased from the local general store. Sixty years later I can still remember the smell of those apples. Red. Succulent. Wonderful. Along with this treasure was a yearly case of prune plums and at Christmas a box of mandarin oranges. That was about the extent of our "store bought" fruit.

Our diet, however, did not lack fruit as the area surrounding our homestead was as rich and varied as any orchard. Raspberries, choke cherries, cranberries, blueberries, and Saskatoons were there for the picking. And pick we did. By the end of every September Mom had several hundred quarts of wild berries on her cellar shelves.

Saskatoons were one of the last wild crops of summer. The good patch was a family secret and several miles away, so once a year dad would harness up the team and the women of the family would gather up washtubs, cream cans, and every available bucket. Then, with jam cans tied around our waists, we would head to the secret patch. Pick those berries. Fill those jars.

In December when a northern blizzard blew snow through the moss-chinked logs of home, nothing warmed the spirits like a hot Saskatoon pie whose fruit had been harvested beneath a golden summer sun.

13 Sandhills

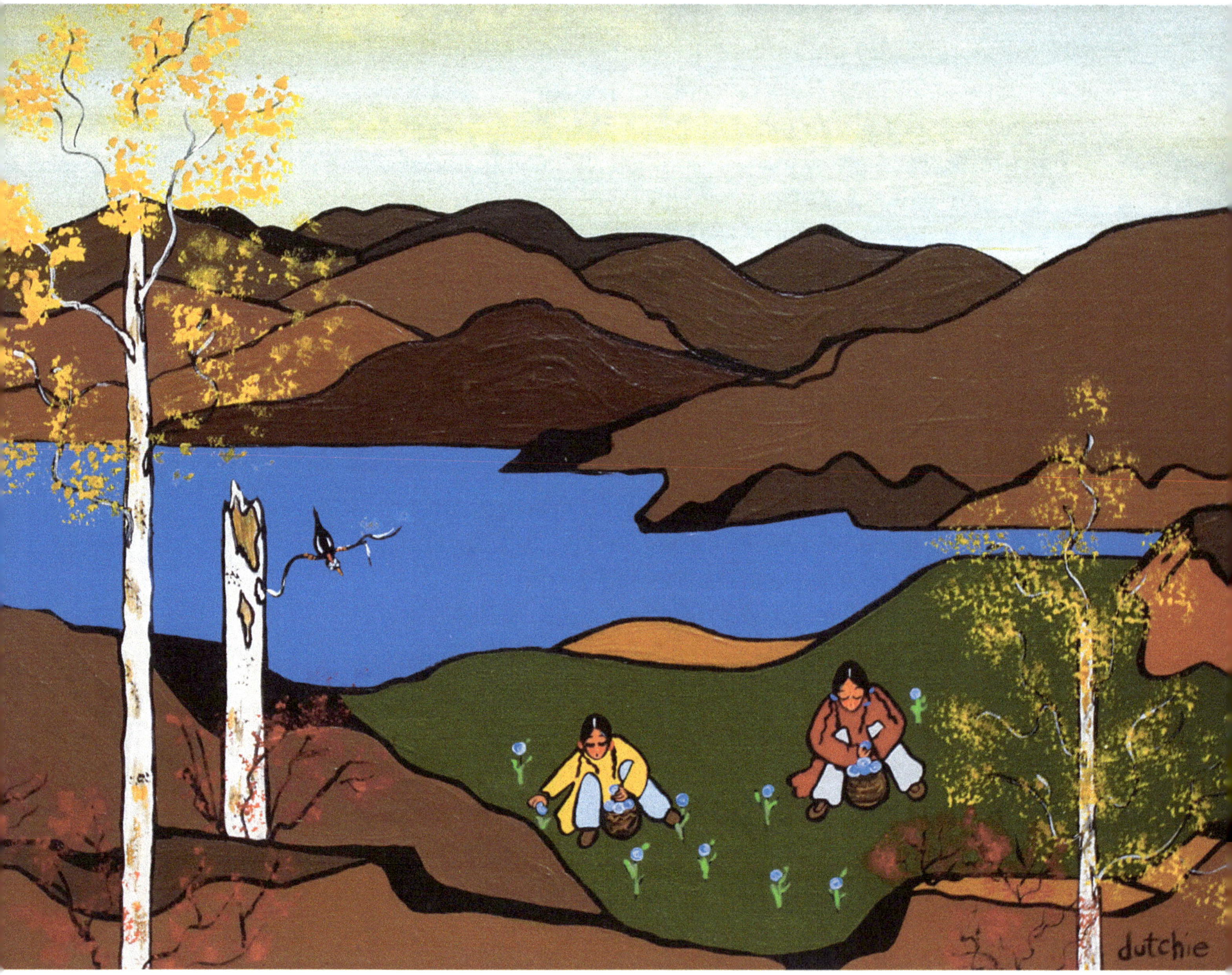

Blueberries
acrylic / canvas
84 x 47 cm

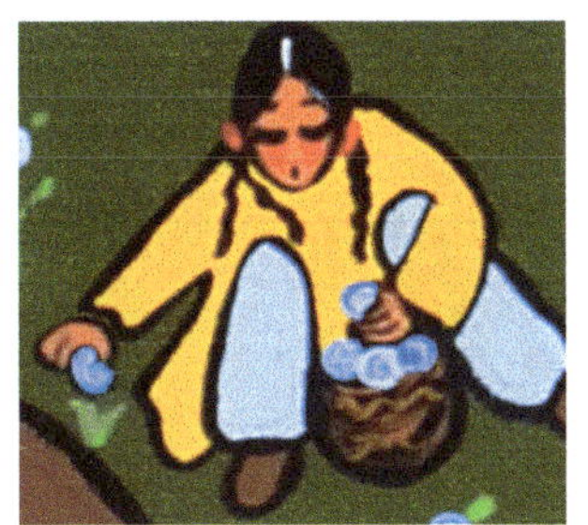

Blueberries and low bush cranberries were the last wild crops of the year. Around the second corner from the home place was what the locals called the sand hills, a rolling area of gentle hills separated by tamarack trees and muskeg. It was there on the sandy slopes that the blueberries grew. The muskeg was filled with tiny, tart cranberries that were miserable as the dickens to pick. These were not favorite berries. It took all day to pick a bucket full, and required an equal amount of sugar to make them palatable. We picked enough for the Christmas and Thanksgiving birds and then looked for greener pastures. Back up the slopes to the blueberry patch.

We shared these hills willingly with the local town folk as well as the Woodland Cree, who would pitch their teepees and stay for days. We could tell by the laughter of both adults and children that it was a joyous time for them too. Sort of a last hurrah before winter set in.

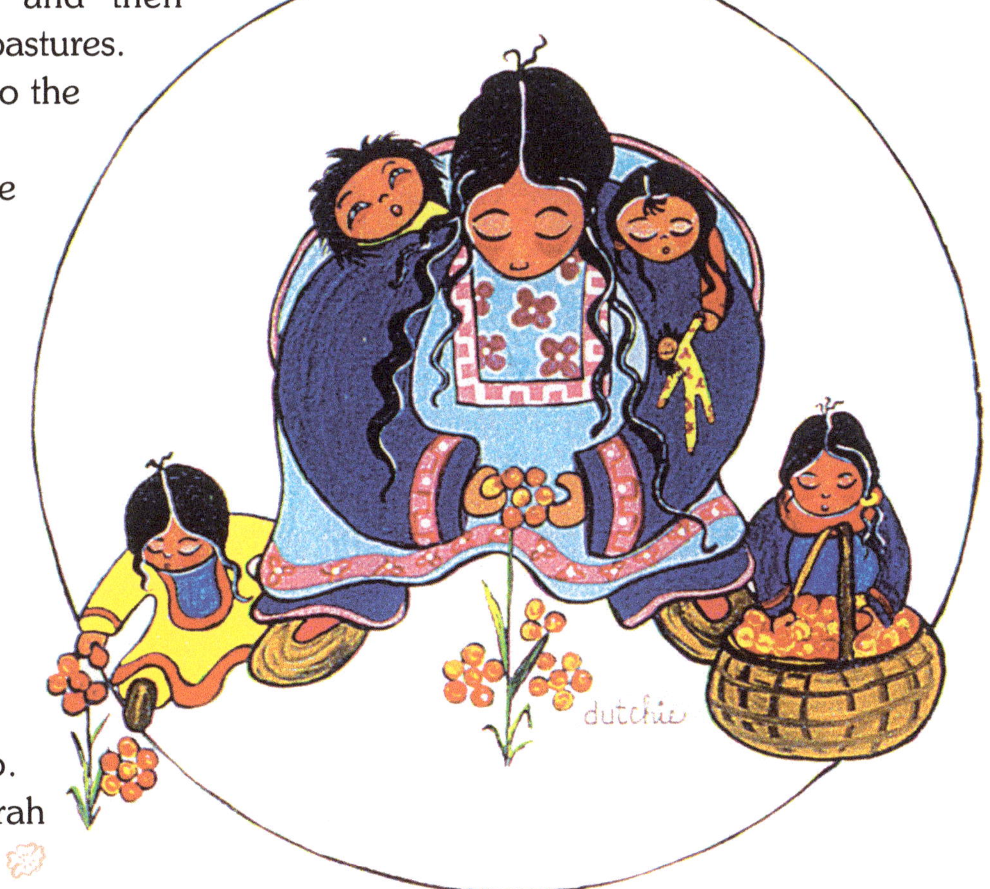

Berry Pickers
acrylic / canvas
29 x 29 cm

14 Winter Wood

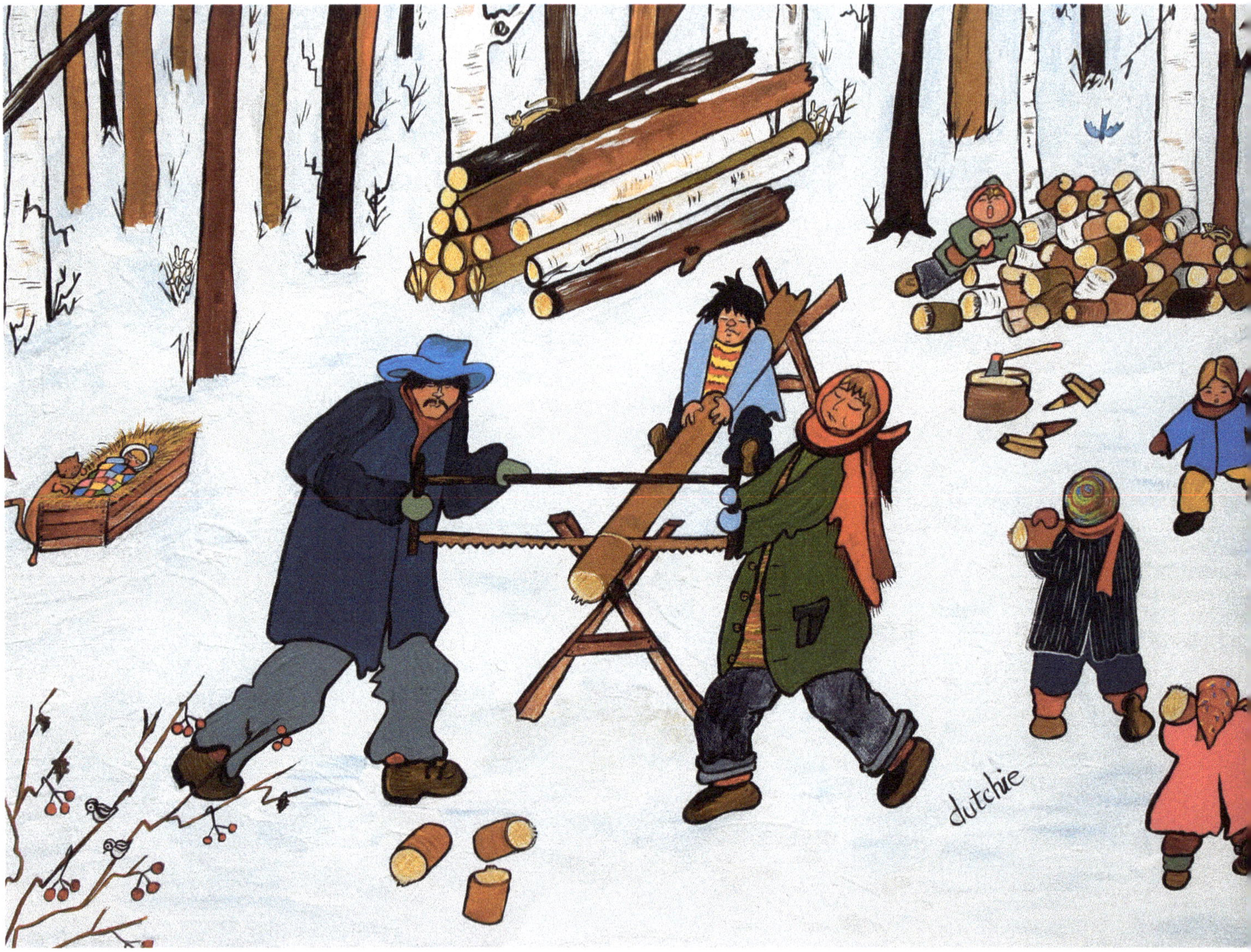

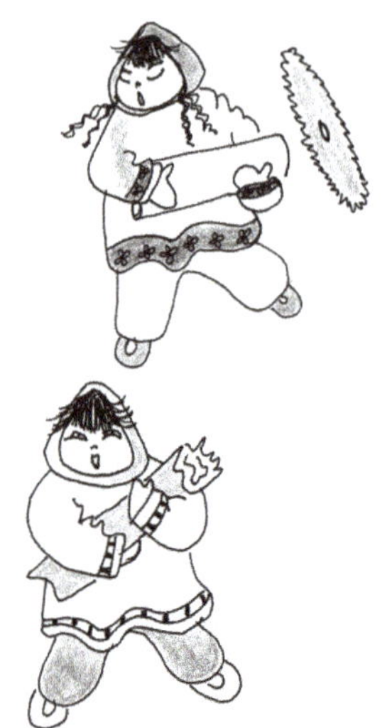

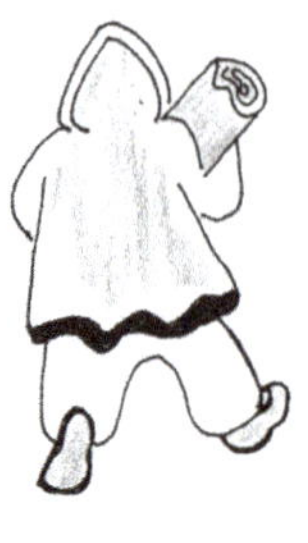

Winter Wood
acrylic / canvas
61 x 77 cm

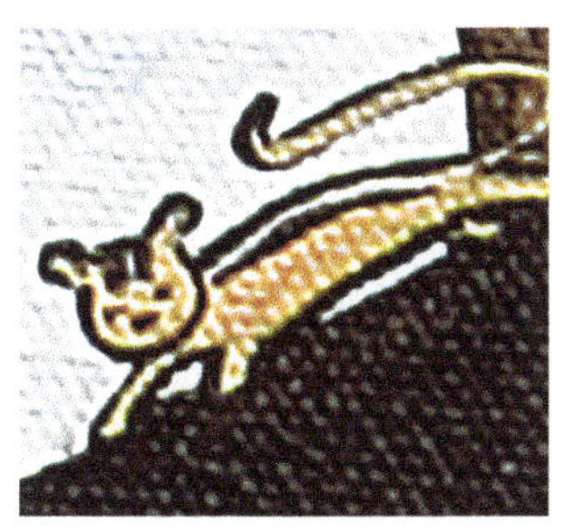

In September the days shortened and the nights turned cold. Winter's first breath could be felt across the valley. It reminded us that summer was over. The winter season was upon us. We'd best be ready.

The green vegetables died with the first frost; the tops of the potatoes lay limp on the ground, dead, except for the harvest beneath the rich soil. The sheaves in the field had been threshed. Grain was taken to the elevator or stored for fodder; the hay dried and stacked. The last berry crop was safely canned and lined cellar shelves. The homesteaders in the valley were ready for the dark days of winter.

Winter darkness, brightened only by coal oil lamps and a few hours of sunlight, settled across the land. It was a time to enjoy the fruits of summer's labor. Keep the wood box full. Eat hearty. Dress warmly.

Winter's work was at a slower pace than the dog days of summer, nonetheless there was still a lot to do. The things I remember most were the long icicles hanging from the mouths and noses of the cattle. When we forked hay into the corral they would lick, with warm tongues, trying desperately to "defrost" so that they could eat.

I remember the cold walks to and from school. We were allowed to miss only if the mercury dropped below minus forty degrees. Strangely enough we were always disappointed when this happened, and usually just donned an extra pair of socks and hit the trail.

It's not hard to recall the mournful howl of the timber wolves as they gathered in the valleys, the nervous bawl of cattle, and the bark of the dog as he put up a brave front.

I'll never forget the image of Mom bent over a frozen side of beef that was stored in a granary. She used a saw to free up a piece of meat to cook for dinner. The thick "sawdust" of meat and bone slowed the blade but, when gathered and hung on the clothesline in a cheesecloth ball, was great food for the winter birds.

The steamy smell of a barn that had housed the milk cows and horses against the night cold was pungent but not unpleasant. The horses would nicker gently as we squeezed between fat bodies to give them their morning oats. The cows were never as grateful. They would swat you with urine soaked tails at milking time and fill your hair with their fleas. Never expect an ounce of gratitude out of a country cow.

Barn cats, on the other hand, rubbed scraggy bodies against your jeans and waited patiently for fresh milk to be squirted directly into their open mouths. If you like to be thanked for your labor take an old barn cat over an ornery cow any time.

Homes in the valley were heated with wood. There are no words to describe the importance of a huge woodpile in northern Canada prior to the 1950s. We simply could not have survived the bitter cold without many cords of the stuff. It was our only source of heat and cooking fuel. Armloads of wood, covered with ice and snow, were packed into the house daily.

Gathering timber for fuel was one of the major jobs of winter. Dad gathered the trees from crown land outside the homestead limits. He hand chopped and limbed the trees, loaded them onto a horse drawn sleigh, and brought them home. This was always done in the winter as it was a very time-consuming job. Also, muskeg could only be crossed when it was frozen and Dad needed to cross several areas of muskeg to get to the best trees.

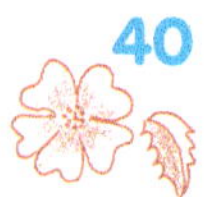

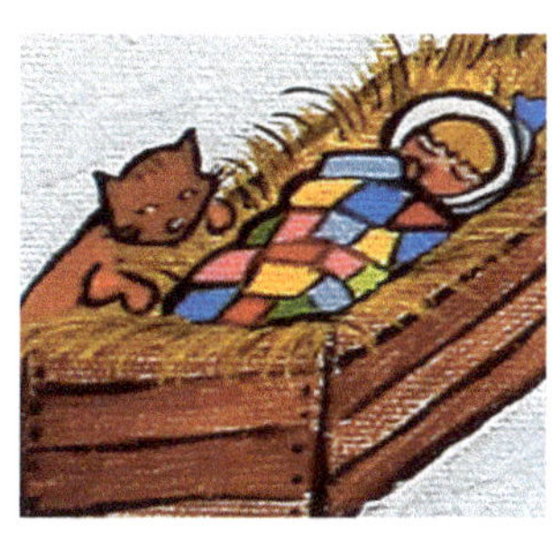

Our wood was always harvested a year in advance. It was cut green and had to dry before it would burn efficiently. Once home it was the job of the entire family to cut and stack the wood. It took a long time to cut a tree by hand into stove-sized blocks. Dad finally traded his labor for our neighbor's saw that was hooked by a long belt to an old steel wheeled tractor. A huge saw, about forty inches in diameter, would spin loudly and at great speed. Dad would feed the logs into the saw and we kids would hang on to the blocks until they dropped and then pack them to the woodpile. I was so afraid of that thing. I always worried that I would misjudge and lose more than just a finger. I much preferred the bucksaw.

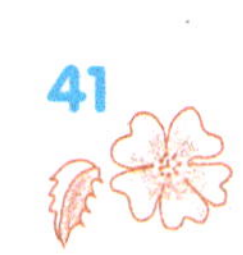

15 Dad's Cows

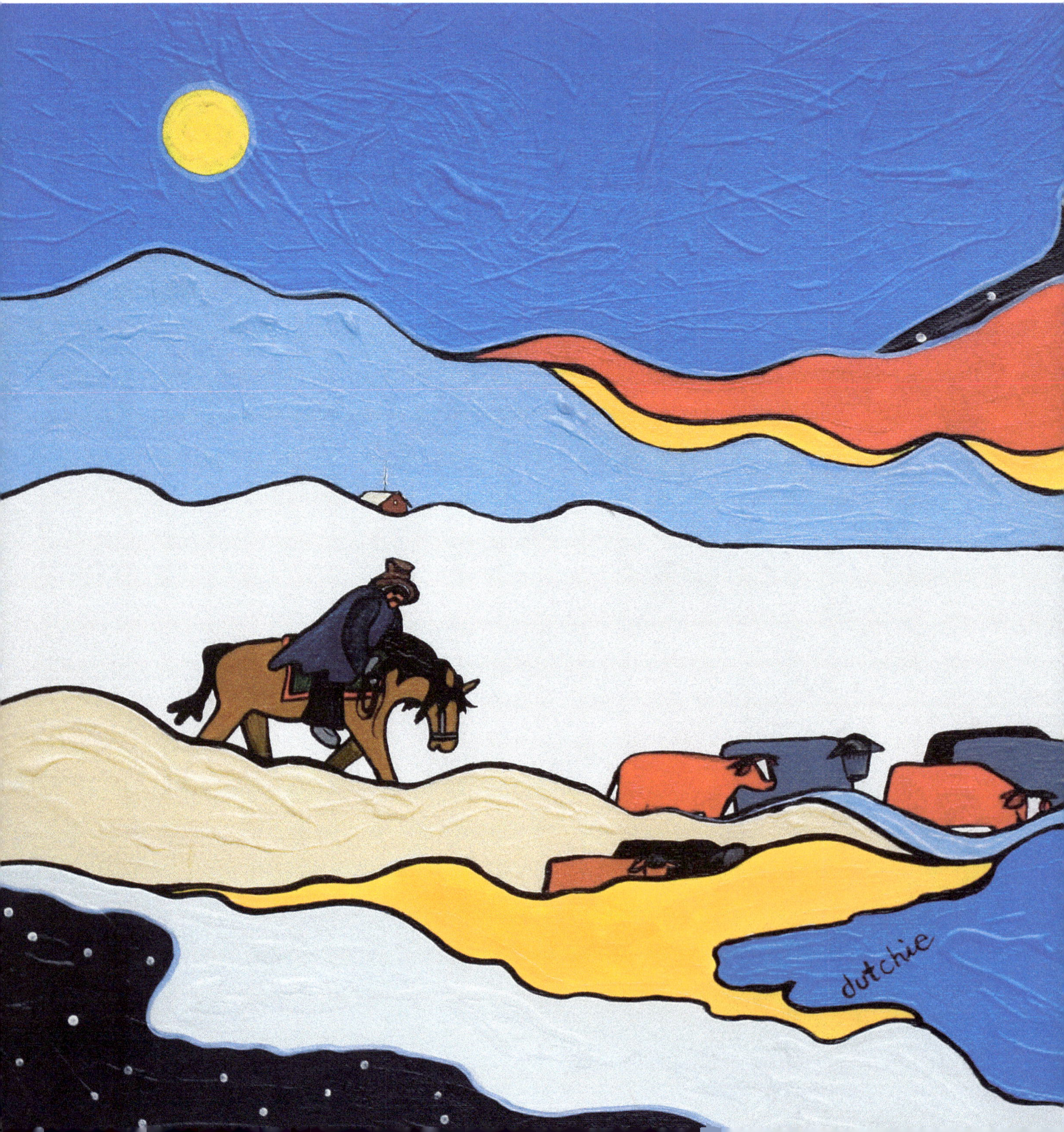

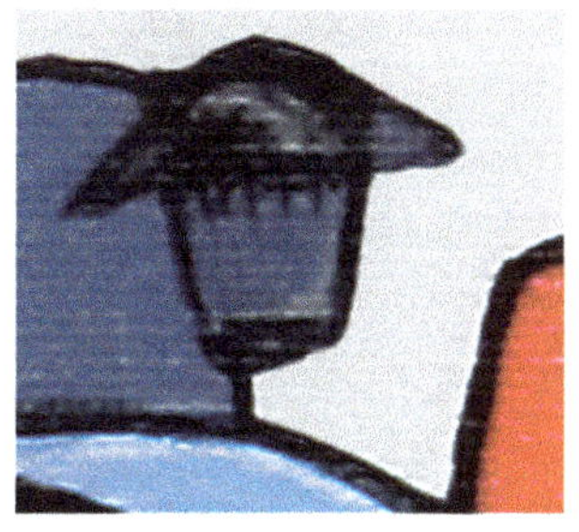

By October the valley lay covered with a thick blanket of snow. The deer and moose pawed at the frozen earth to uncover the frozen tufts of grass that lay beneath the snow. The wolves would stalk nearby, waiting. Waiting for an animal weakened by lack of grazing to fall. It made their job easier.

On the farm our job got harder as it was time to round up the cattle and bring them home. There we would have to feed them daily until they could return to the pastures in the spring.

Digging through old photos I found a black and white snap of Dad "bringing home the cows." It got my memories flowing and I painted the picture of Dad as he brought the cows home to winter.

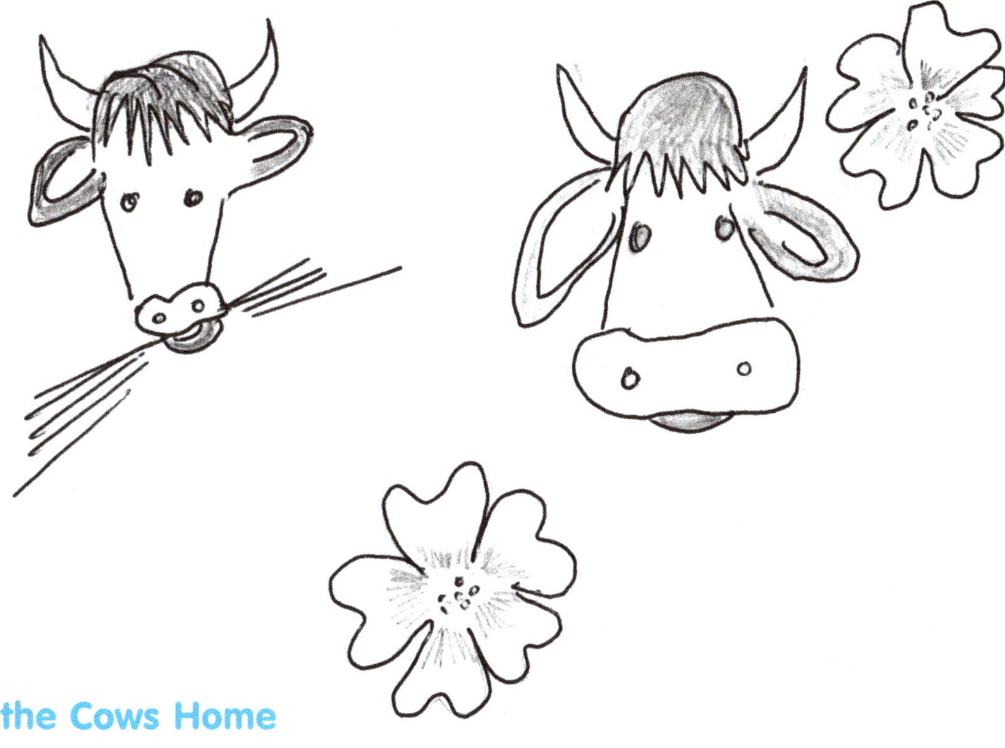

Bringing the Cows Home
acrylic / canvas
66 x 51 cm

16 Storyteller

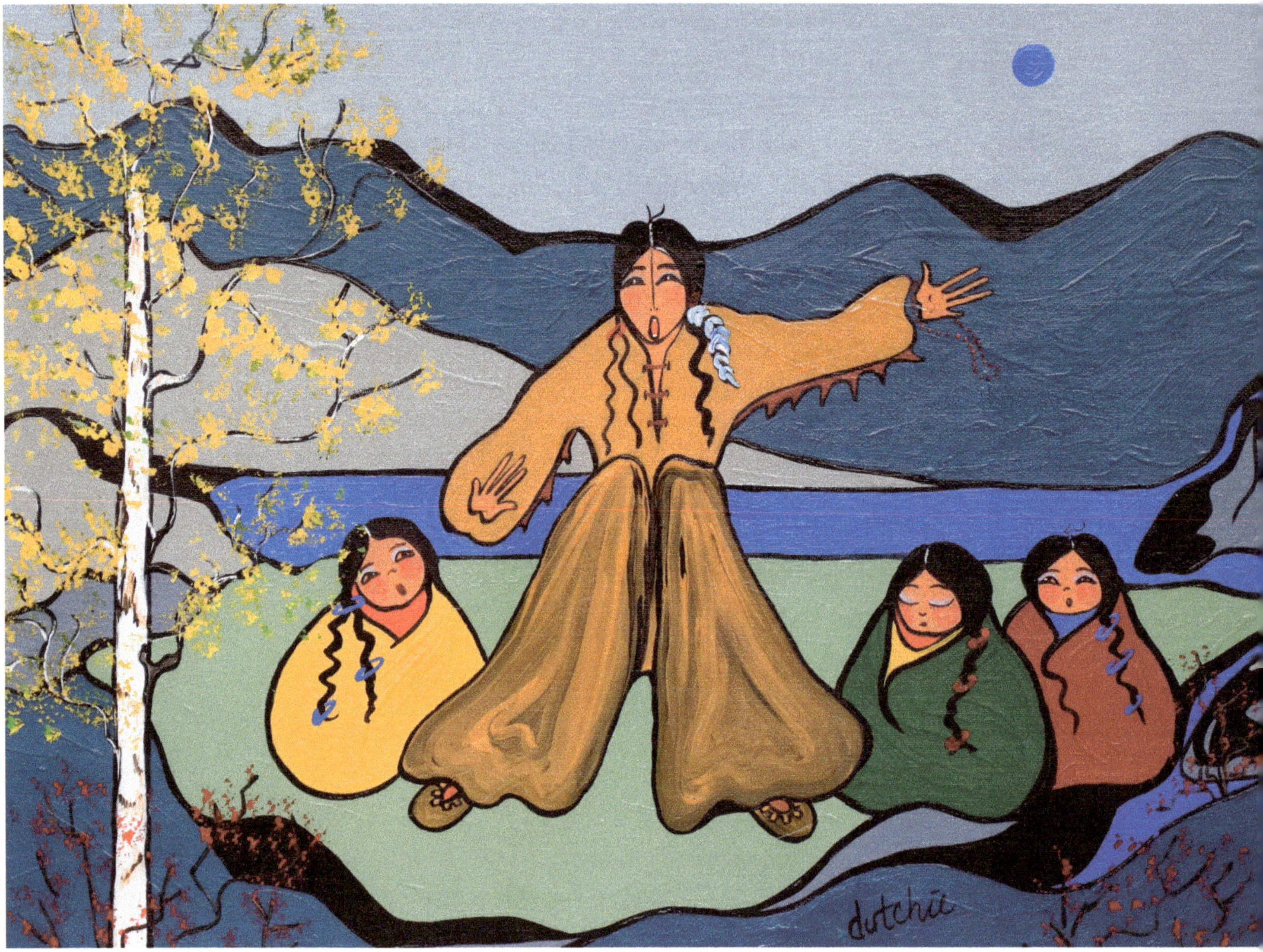

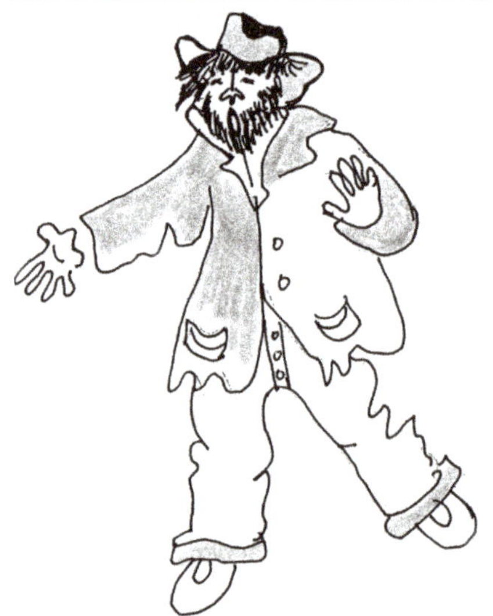

Storyteller
acrylic / canvas
59 x 44 cm

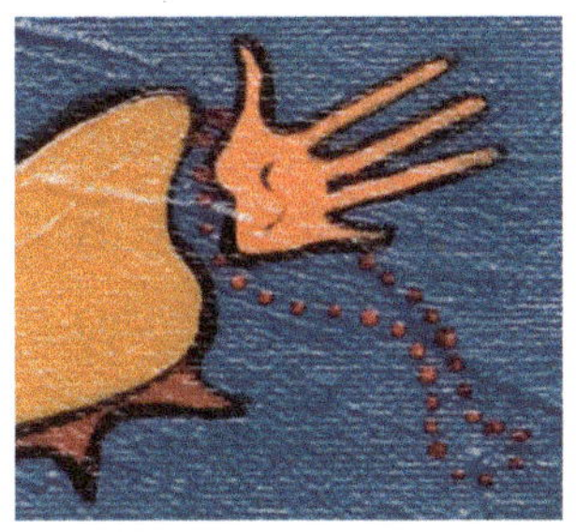

In the depth of winter's darkness we learned to entertain ourselves. By the light of coal oil lamps we dressed dolls that we had cut out of the Eaton's catalogue, played pick-up-sticks, rolled plasticene into wonderful figurines, and played cards. Dad would sit in the evening and play penny poker with us. On a wall in his den he kept a cow horn full of pennies that we would share at the beginning of the game. We learned spit-in-the-middle, jacks and sevens, highball, low ball, kings and little ones, and many other forms of gambling with that horn full of copper coins that was returned to its nail on the wall after every game. We all became adept card sharks by the age of ten!

On rare occasions the sound of sleigh runners told us that company was coming. Dad would go to the gate, open it and welcome our guests. Most of the time they were neighbors. Strangers were equally welcomed; sometimes more so because their pigs had never rooted up our garden or, worse, their mongrel bull had not broken the fence and gotten romantic with Dad's prized Hereford heifers. Nevertheless, all were welcome and, of course, fed before they went on their way. Oft times, over many cups of strong tea, they would linger and visit. It was at these times that I learned the value of a good storyteller.

Our valley was an electricity-free territory. The odd battery radio in the valley occasionally brought the news of the outside world: the up-coming war, the price of grain, what Hitler and Mussolini were up to. I think they all shared equal importance. The war, to me, was a bunch of hungry kids "over there" who would love to have that crust of bread I had been caught sneaking to the dog. Besides these few occasions of radio news, we lived in blissful isolation from the hardships of the war and the rest of the world.

Our stories were of a much more immediate nature.

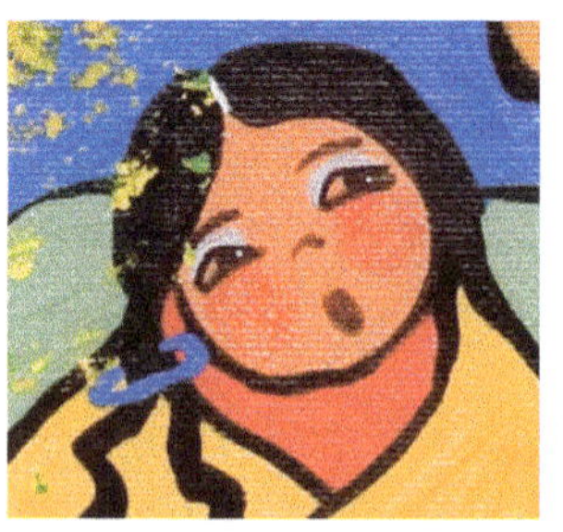

A guest to our home meant news of the valley. It was at these times that we learned whose cow had fallen through the ice, and which newly wedded couple only needed six months to make a baby. The answer to that always was, "Well for darn sure the next six will take nine months." Chuckle, chuckle, chuckle. Then, on to how the trapping was and, always, the weather.

Every story was embellished from neighbor to neighbor. Our home was one of the more isolated in the valley, so by the time a story reached our fireside it had only taken three months to make a baby, six prize milk cows had fallen through the ice, the trapping was the worst it had been since the late 1800s and "all that darn testing of those "nuculeer" weapons was sure as heck going to change the weather patterns and ensure crop failures, yes siree!"

Valley gossip was laced with humor and wisdom. Stories past and present were told with gusto and exaggeration. While I make light of the storytellers and the tales I heard, "while not being heard," I learned much around the pot-bellied stove listening to my dad and our guests.

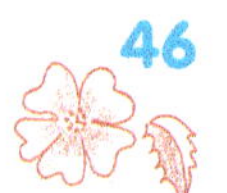

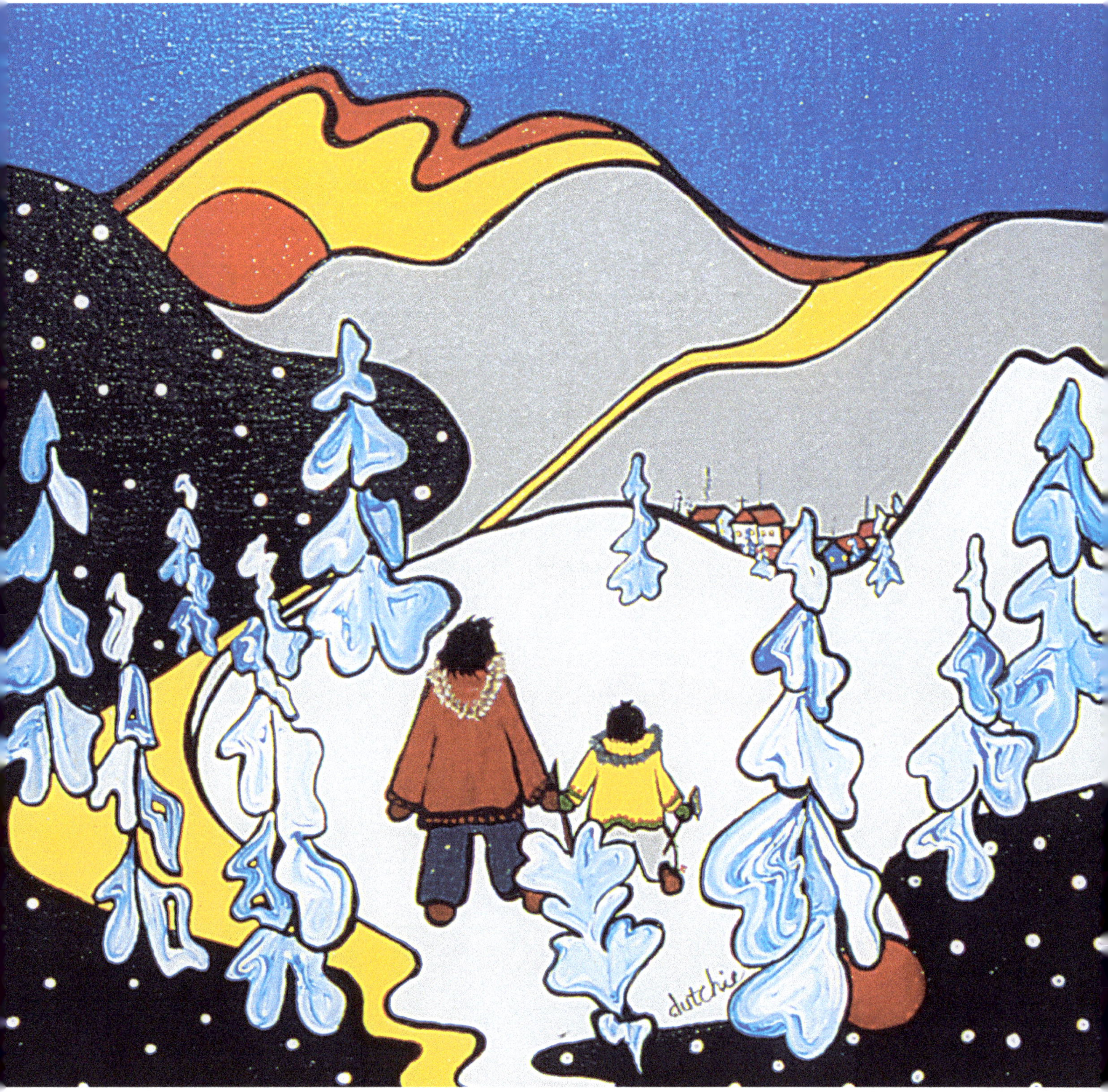

Xmas Tree

acrylic / canvas

36 x 41 cm

Collection: Pat and Robin O'Reilley

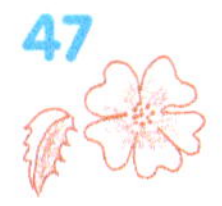

17 Prairie Chickens

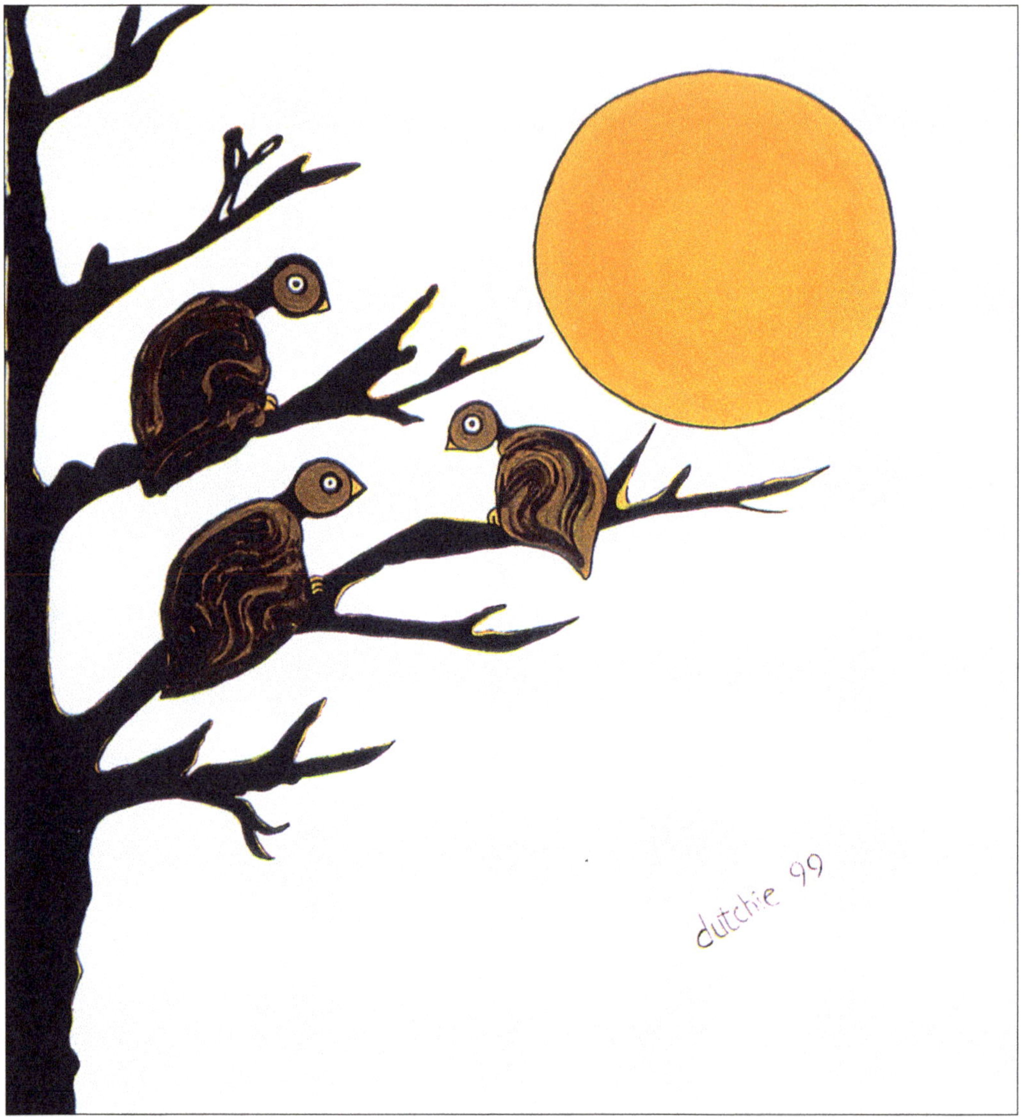

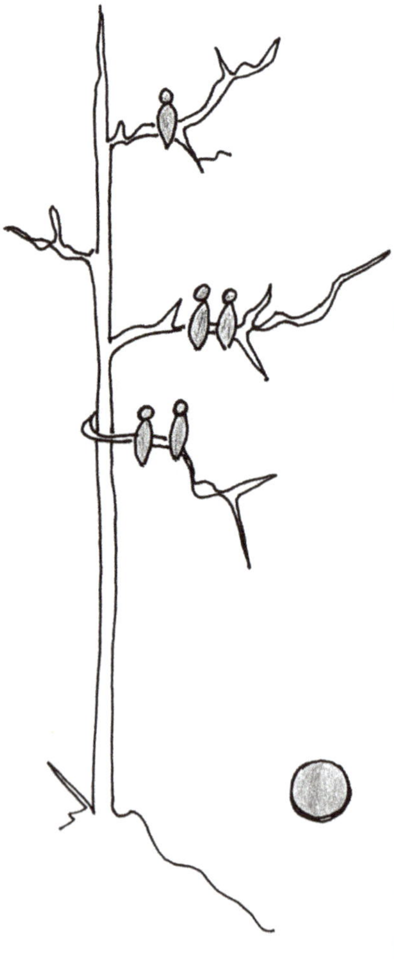

Prairie Chickens

acrylic / canvas

44 x 49 cm

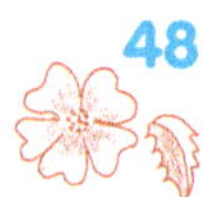

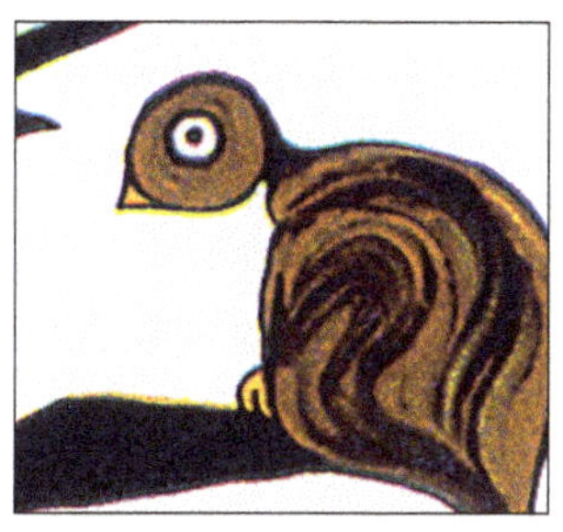

One of the gifts of winter was that on very cold days the prairie chickens would roost in the leafless trees just before the sun set. There, outlined against a barren background, they would huddle against the cold. Sometimes a dozen or more would use the same tree as their nighttime refuge against predators.

On windless nights when the mercury dropped below twenty degrees, and the prairie chickens ruffled their feathers against the cold, my sister or I would take the .22 rifle and try to get some variety into our diets. Their tender white breasts and legs, along with veggies from the cellar, made a wonderful stew. I remember how proud Mom would always make me feel when I came home with two or three chickens. I knew that I had contributed to the family unit every time my bullet found its mark.

Dad, who was quite a philosopher, taught me many lessons. One I've never forgotten. It was early July; I had taken the .22 with me when I went for a walk. Homeward bound, I spotted a prairie chicken running across the road. I swung the rifle to my shoulder. Took aim and fired. I proudly took the bird home, expecting praise.

Dad said very softly, "That's a fine looking bird you've got there, Duchess. I hope the coyotes don't eat her babies tonight."

Silence. I stood waiting — waiting for a word that would help ease the guilt. He turned and without a word walked away.

I couldn't eat the chicken stew that night. And I never shot another prairie chicken during spring and summer months.

We never went hungry on the farm. The land provided and we reaped her gifts. We learned that "to all things there is a season." We gathered only what we needed and the prairie chickens resting in the tree near our home during the spring and summer months were safe from well-aimed bullets.

18 Sawmill

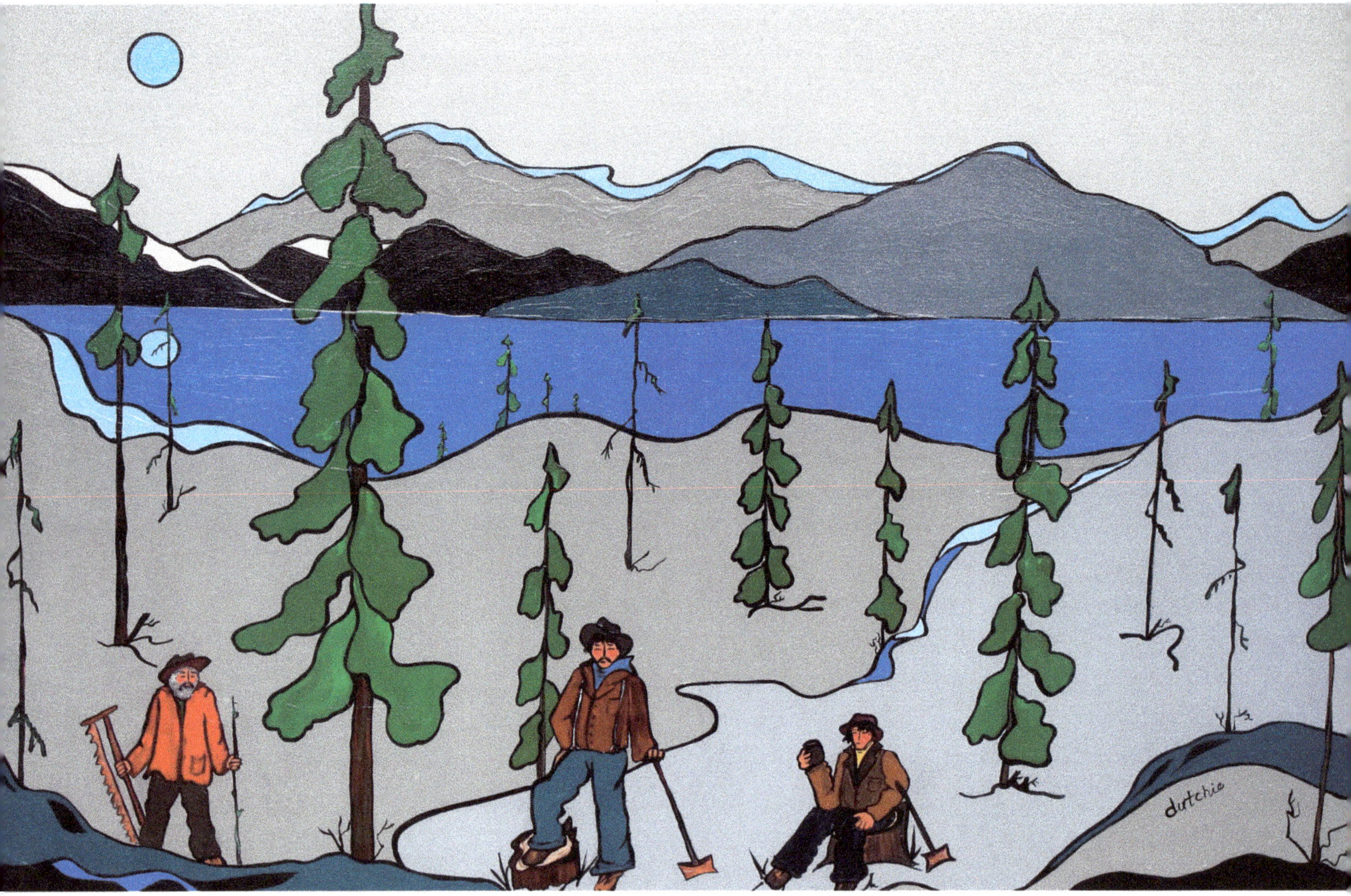

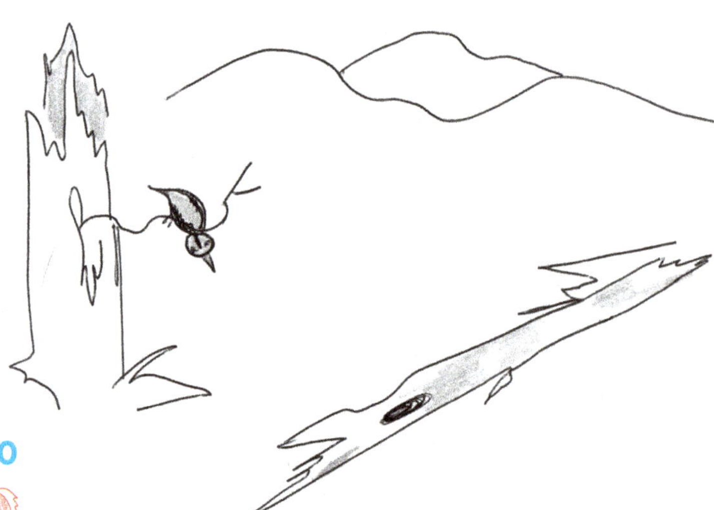

Lumberjacks

acrylic / canvas

58 x 91 cm

Collection: Slave Lake Chamber of Commerce

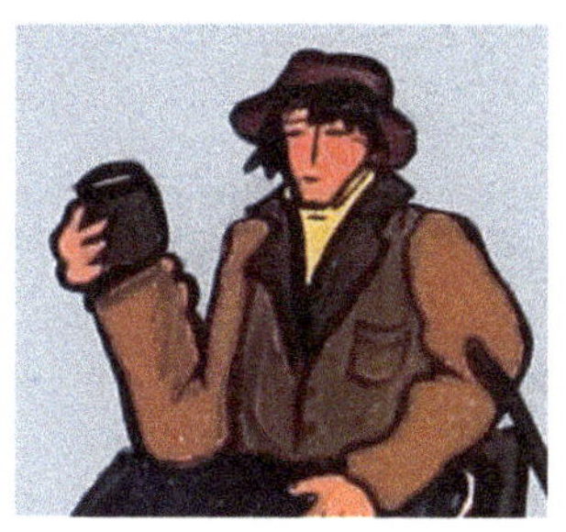

Farming in the valley was a way of life, not a livelihood. My dad, and most valley men, left their farms for several months in the winter to seek employment. They had no choice. They had to develop their homesteads to government standards or they would never receive the deed to the land.

My dad chose to work in forestry as a way to earn money to keep his farm. Every winter he would leave the valley to run a sawmill in Slave Lake. This left tending the livestock and raising six kids to Mom.

The hard work, the winter darkness, the isolation; I can't imagine how lonely she must have been. And still, aside from frozen toes and noses, I remember winter as a time of peace and solitude. We had food, shelter, clothing. And most of all we had Mom.

Dad would return to the farm when the spring winds thawed the earth making it impossible to log the muskeg. The season of planting and reaping the harvest of the land was once more alive in the valley, made possible by Dad running a sawmill in the winter months and Mom running the farm. We always said Dad went to work in the winter. I don't think we had a name for what Mom did. We simply knew that Mom stayed home and that seemed to say it all.

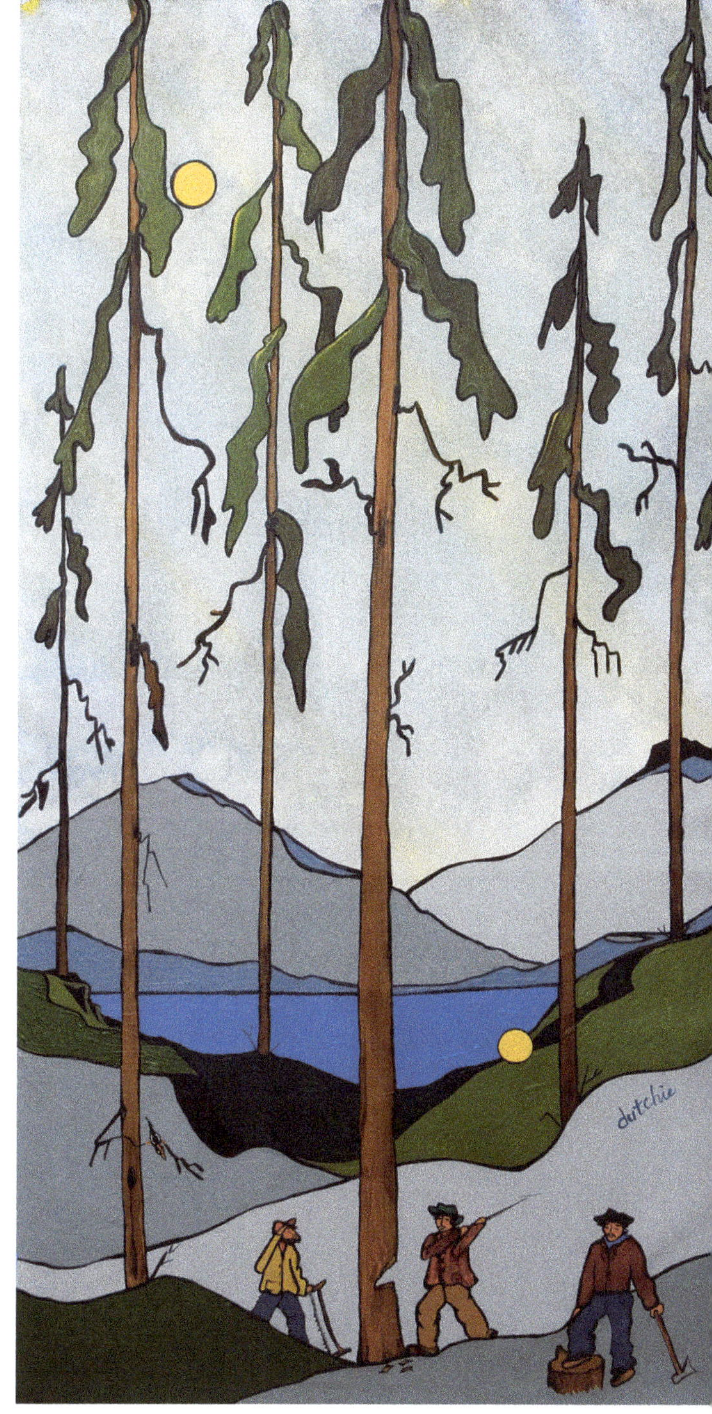

Dad and the Sinclair Boys

acrylic / canvas

51 x 91 cm

Collection: Slave Lake Chamber of Commerce

19 Mother's Child

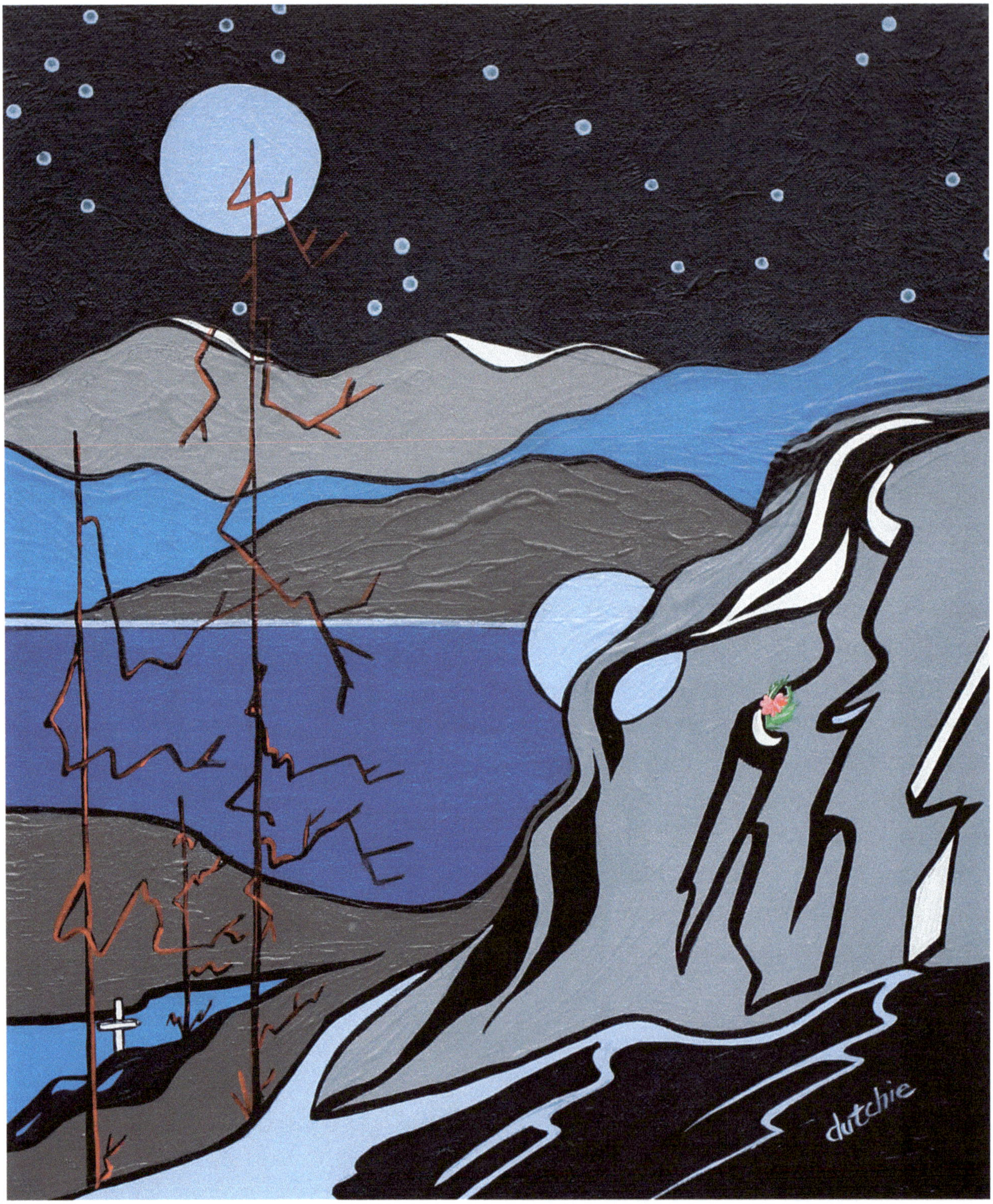

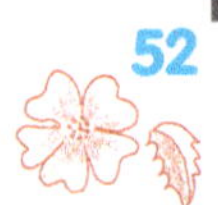

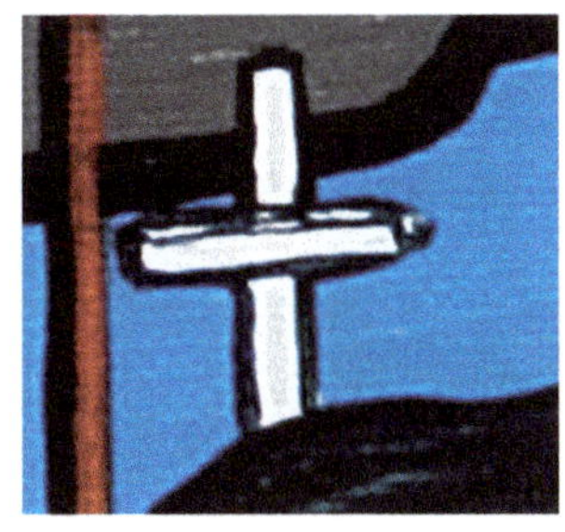

Death is universal and grief is no respecter of time or place. Our valley was not exempt, and had its share of sadness. I was reminded of this several years ago. I was trekking north of Lesser Slave Lake, enjoying the solitude and memories of childhood when I happened upon a small cross nestled among the deep underbrush. It was a small child's grave, as rocks outlined where a mound of earth once lay.

Too often I had passed the symbols of other people's sadness and felt, not empathy, but gratitude for the gift of life. I could not, however, dismiss this rough-hewn cross. No name. No date. Both long since erased by time. I stood many minutes as sadness overcame me and tears filled my eyes. I knew that no matter how long ago, a mother had lovingly placed her child in this bleak wilderness and had felt the pain of all mothers when they bury their babies. I knew that beneath the silken moss of summer and the barren snows of winter lay some mother's child.

We lost our son to cancer recently. Therefore, *Some Mother's Child* was very difficult for me to paint. However, I knew that not to tell this story would be as corrosive as the northern winds, for it would dismiss all the forgotten crosses that make up such a large part of our northern heritage.

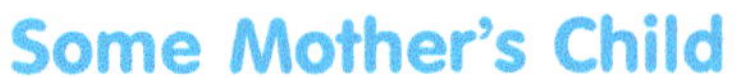

Some Mother's Child

acrylic / canvas

66 x 51 cm

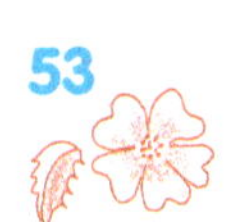

20 Mabel's Baby

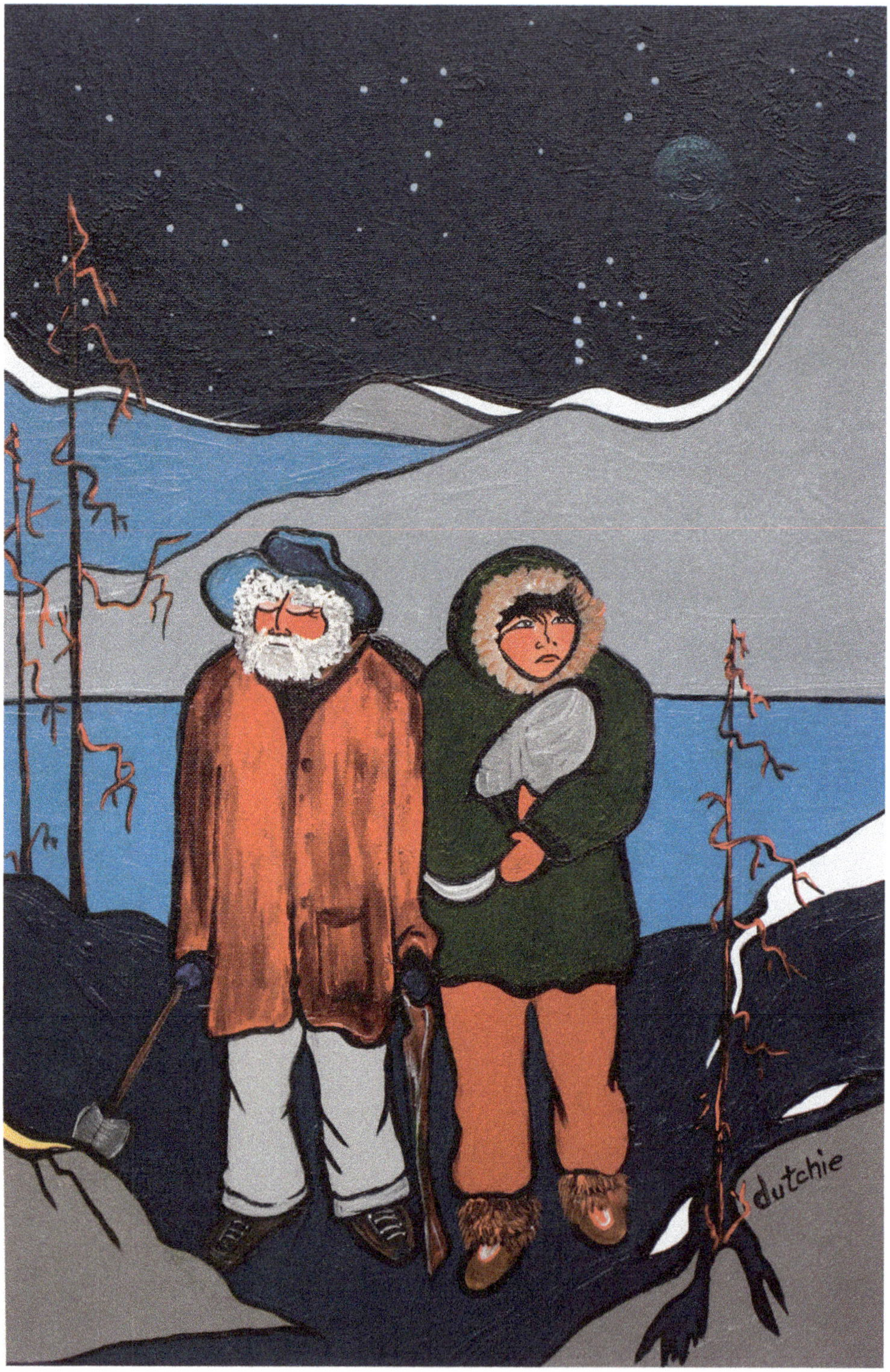

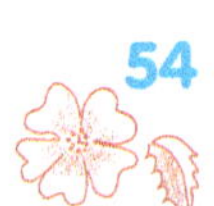

Mabel's Baby tells another sad story of the harshness of northern isolation.

I remember it was a bitter cold night. The wind howled through the tamarack trees and whistled through the cracks in our log home. It was dark. A knock on the door took Dad from his bed. A rimed covered stranger, his face alee to the wind, stood on our step. In his arms, he tenderly held a small swaddled bundle.

"I need an ice pick or shovel," he stated.

When Dad inquired why, our visitor replied, "Mabel's baby died last night."

In silence Dad put on his hat and coat and followed our guest into the night.

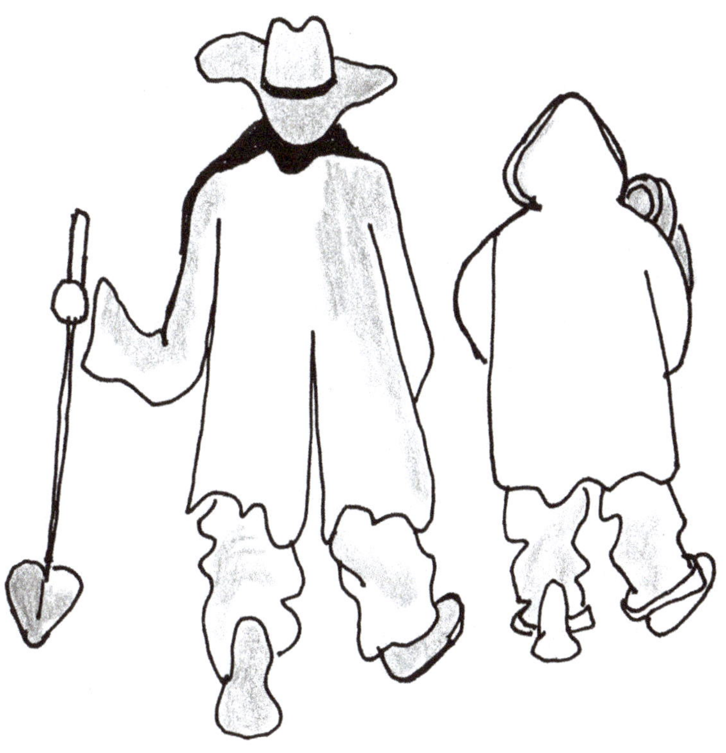

Mabel's Baby

acrylic / canvas

65 x 51 cm

Collection: Brenda Kelemen-Tkachuk

21 Mom's Bedroom

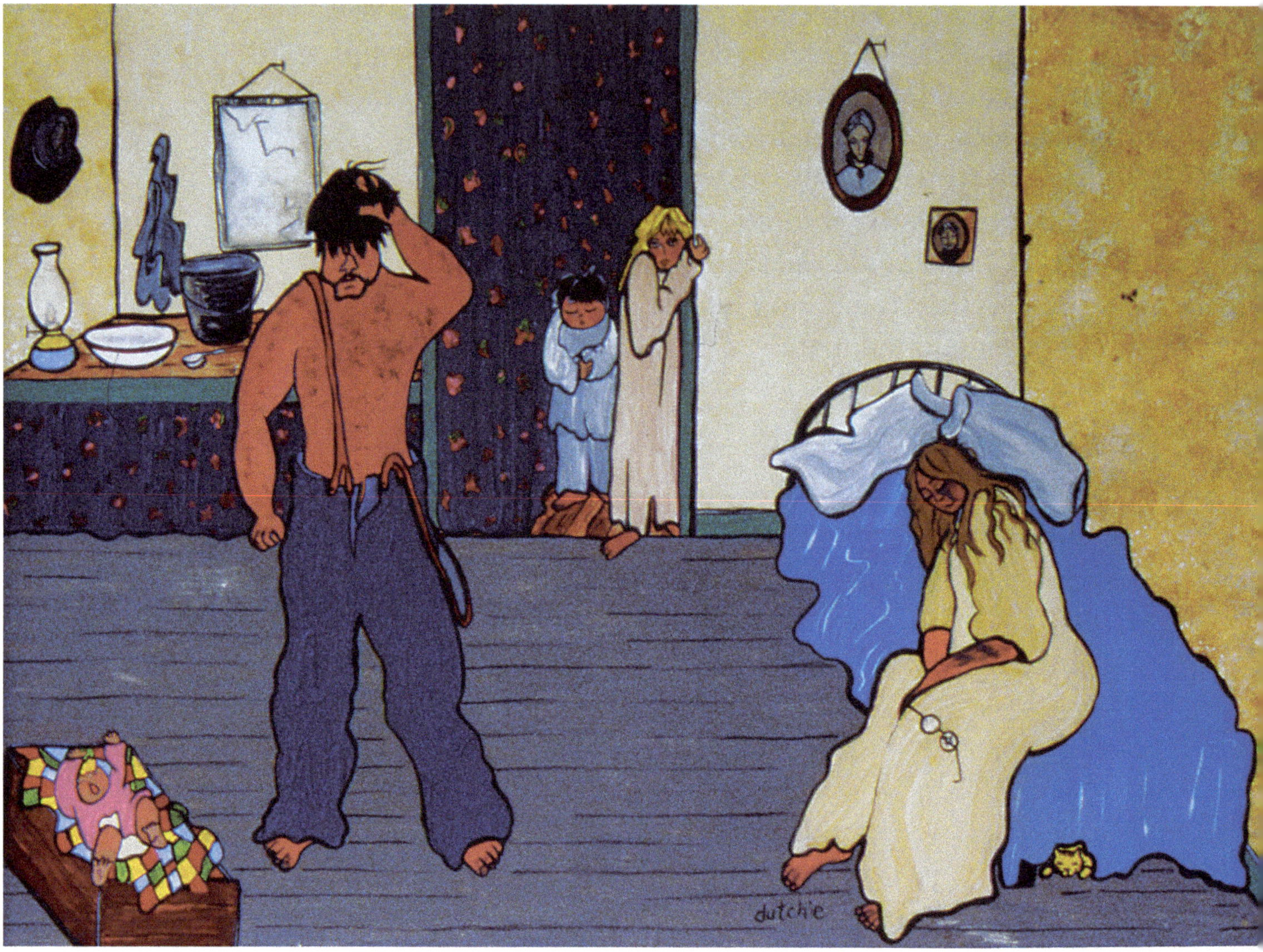

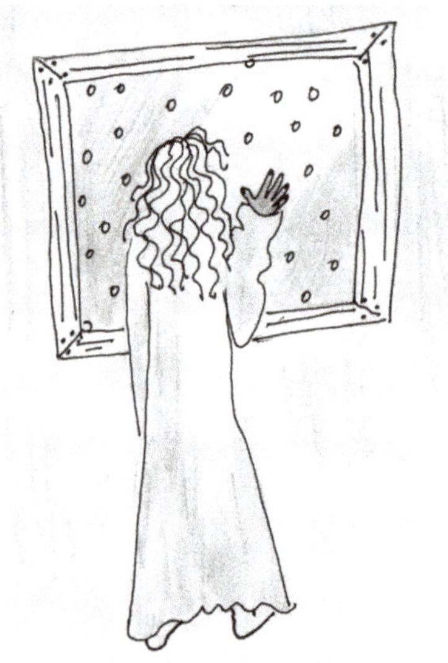

My Mother's Bedroom

acrylic / canvas

66 x 51 cm

Collection: Eric and Patricia Peura

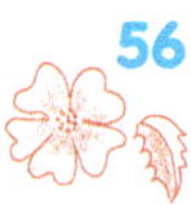

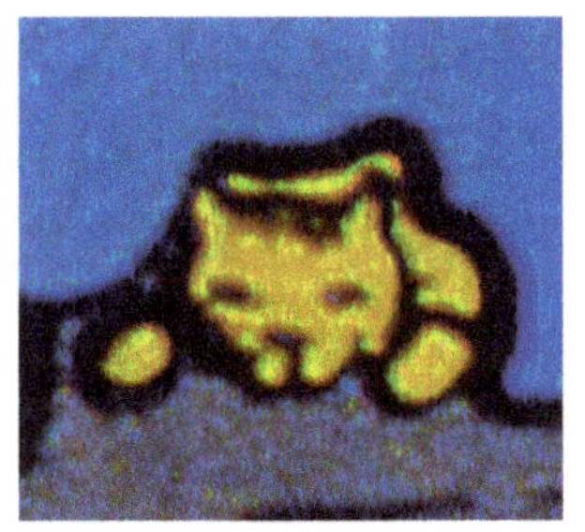

Death was not the only tragedy that lingered in the Valley of the Swan. Sadness and despair take many forms.

I was five or six years old when I watched the horse-drawn sleigh disappear around the first corner, taking my dad across the windswept fields, beyond the frozen muskeg where the birch trees stood. Gone for a day of hand falling trees for our fuel. As the sleigh disappeared from view, my child's heart wished he would die out there in the cold and never come home again.

More than one half a century has passed since that cold winter morning. I know there is never an excuse for domestic violence. I do now, however, understand the harsh conditions under which my parents lived, and how those hardships could nourish anger and fear.

My dad is now 93 years old. His eyes still sparkle. He occasionally calls me by my mom's name. His best memories are of the farm. Occasionally his Irish temper surfaces. I no longer fear him. I hug him. We are at peace, my dad and I. He did his best. Now I wish him life.

I hesitated to hang the painting *My Mother's Bedroom* when I returned home to celebrate Alberta's Centennial in 2005. I did not want to abase my dad's memory, and yet I felt a need to show my mom's side of the story as some folks criticized her harshly for gathering up her six kids, loading the horse and wagon with her belongings, and leaving my dad in 1949.

I had always been proud of our family, including my dad, who in many ways was a very good man. I thought that Dad's temper was a well-kept family secret. As the folks who had known Mom and Dad gathered to celebrate their centennial with me, I was greatly touched by the many women who came and hugged me and said, "We knew, dear."

For those women, who stood and gazed at the picture *My Mother's Bedroom* for long moments with tears

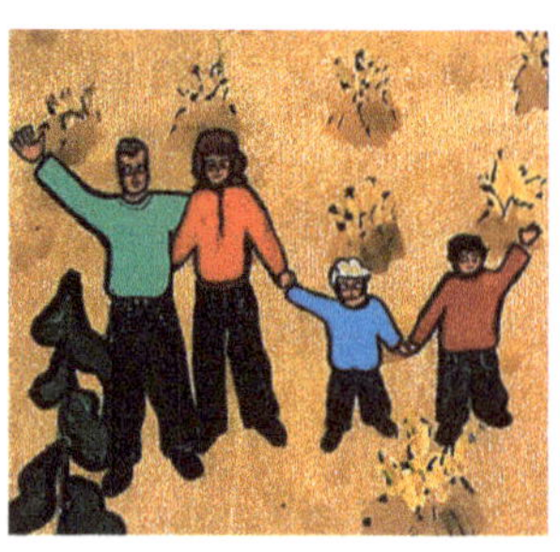

in their eyes, then came to me and said, "Your mom was a wonderful woman." I knew they understood. And so we hugged and cried together and I whispered a silent thank you to my mom, "Thank you for your silent courage, for your leadership by example. I love you, Mom."

Mom was not the only woman to suffer abuse at the hands of her husband. The isolation of our valley and the pride of its women hid many tales of loneliness and abuse. I learned of these stories during my visit home. Certainly they saddened me; mostly, however, I felt relief that perhaps my mom had not suffered alone.

I felt comfort talking with Brenda, a young woman whose grandparents homesteaded northwest of the valley. She and I shared many cups of tea and tears as we recalled the stories of our parents and grandparents. We talked of the hardship, the love, and the ultimate victory over the land.

We laughed as she told of her dad's fear of mice. He was a large man and it became a family joke that he put red jar rings around his pant legs when he went to the fields to keep the "little beggars" from crawling up his trousers. She described how her grandfather, George, plowed around the evergreen trees in the field. Neither Brenda nor I could find a reason for this, as all other trees fell prey to the axe. She said that no wild berry was safe from her mother's berry pail and that she spent every spare moment gathering the saskatoons that grew in abundance around their fields. We understood each other's pain as she talked of her grandfather's physical abuse of his wife, and the lessons we had learned because of this.

Talking with Brenda reminded me of the day Mom left Dad. I think I was ten. I was glad Mom was leaving. Even at that age I knew she could not stay. What I was not expecting was the great loneliness I felt for my dad.

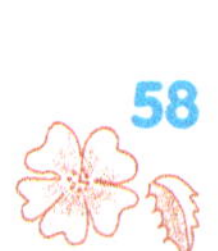

He helped her on to the wagon, shook her hand with great dignity and wished her well. I didn't want Mom to stay. I just didn't want it to be so damned painful. As the wagon rounded the corner taking Mom from the farm, from Dad, from the home she had helped build, I felt such sadness for my dad. I knew Mom would be all right now. I knew my dad would not be. And he wasn't.

May 27, 2004 my dad died at the age of ninety-four. I miss him.

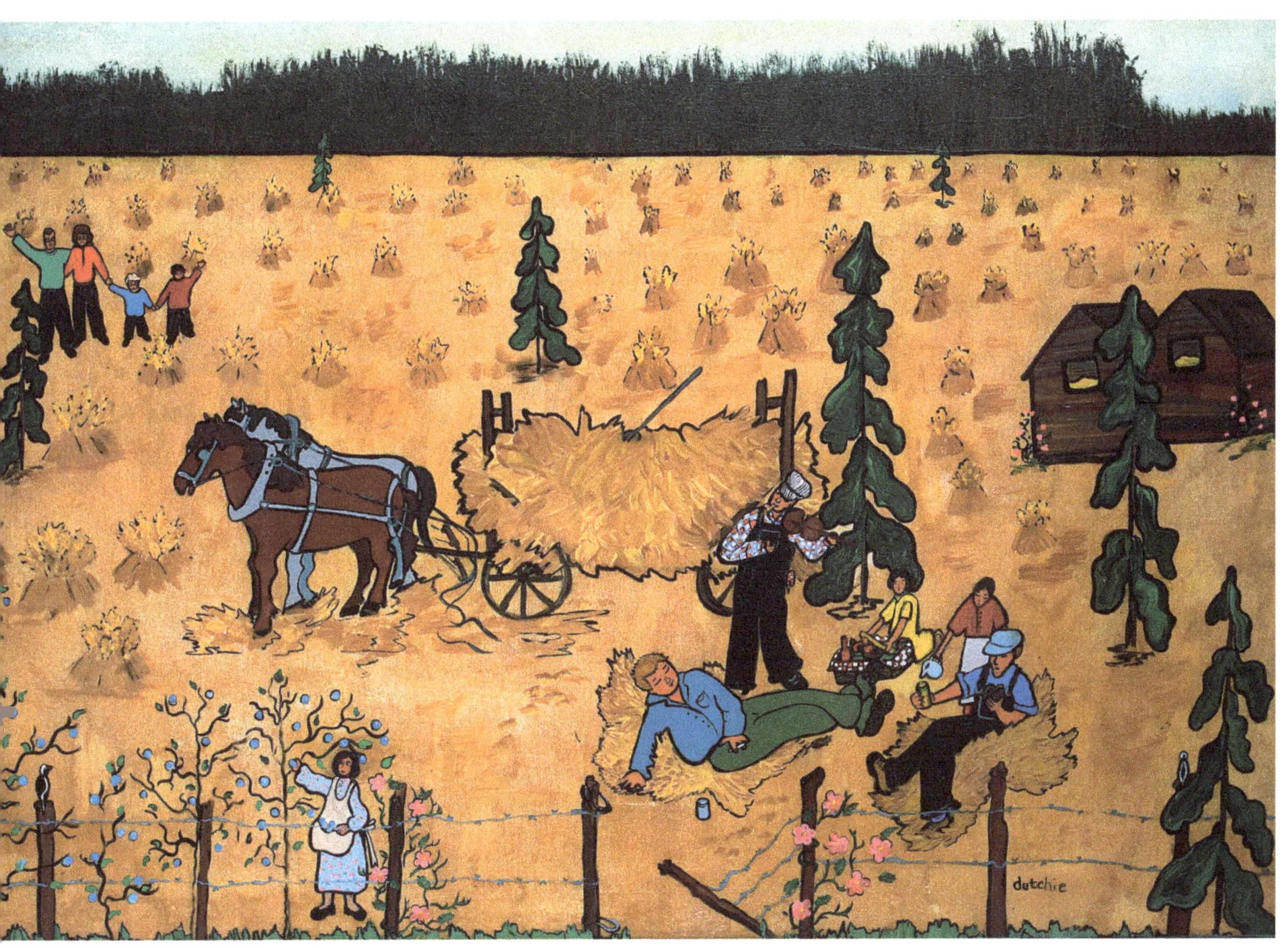

Homestead Memories

acrylic / canvas

76 x 91 cm

Collection: Brenda Kelemen-Tkachuk

22 Ukrainian

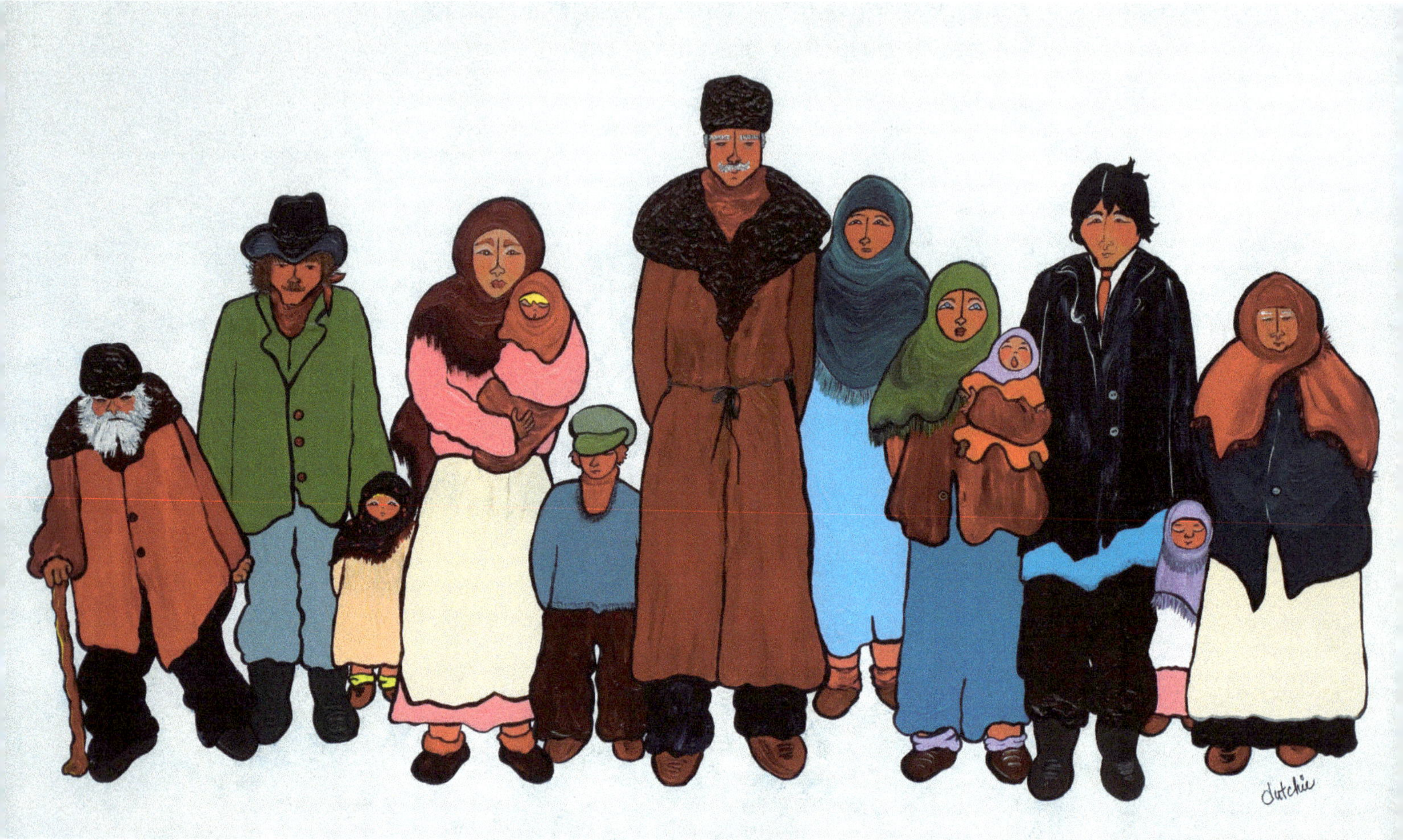

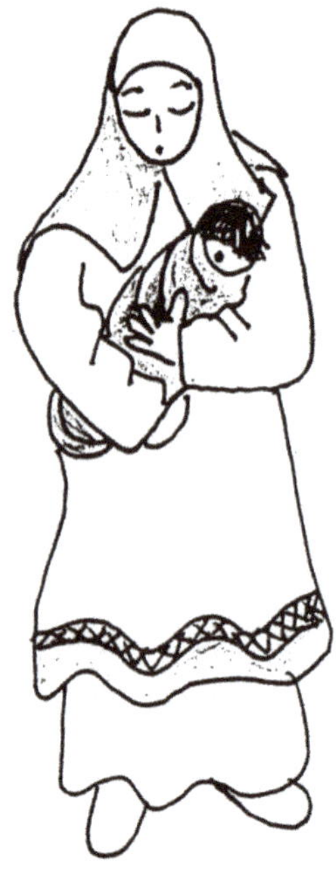

Ukrainian Family
acrylic / canvas
77 x 129 cm

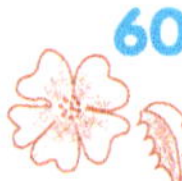

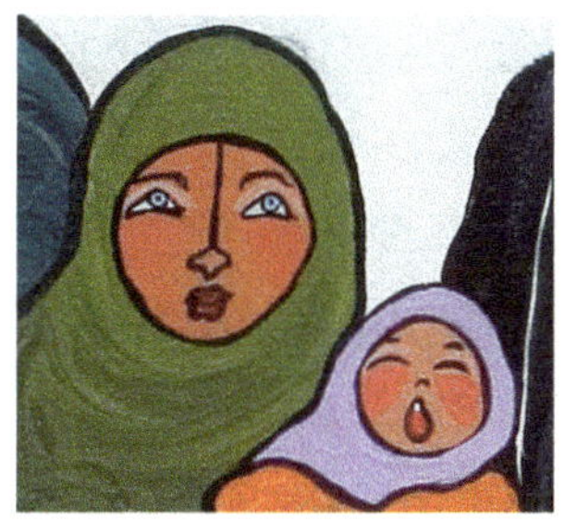

Folks from many parts of the world settled our valley. Each cultural group struggled to keep their homeland traditions while trying to unite and make a strong community. It was not always easy.

I don't recall racial prejudice ever being an issue in our home. My dad scorned laziness, the Catholic Church in Rome, and most politicians. However, never once did I hear him judge a man by his race.

It was when we made our rare trips to town that I saw and felt racial prejudice. A trip into town was always such an adventure. Dad, a proud man, would curry the horses till their coats shone. We kids, with great expectations, would all pile into the wagon. As we entered town we would shyly peek over the sides of the buckboard. Often we would see small groups of "differently" dressed folks eagerly sharing news in a language none of us understood. As a child, I felt the lack of respect accorded them by some of the local townspeople, whose mistrust grew out of misunderstanding and certainly a lack of tolerance for a culture they knew nothing about.

I was reminded of this division of cultures when I toured the Slave Lake area in 2005. I was delighted to find my mom's signature, dated 1951, along with that of other ladies from the valley, on a large hand quilted coverlet displayed on a wall in the Kinusayo Museum. Considering the proportionally large population of Ukrainian families in the valley, the small number of female Ukrainian names on

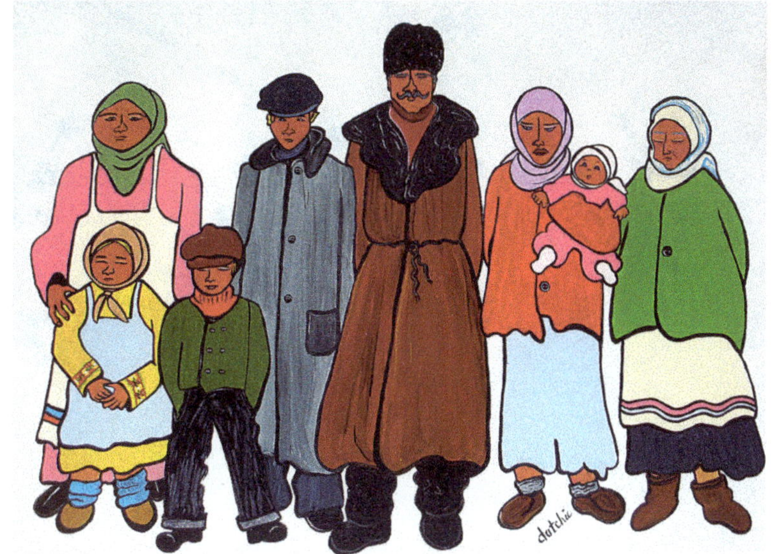

Ukrainian Neighbours
acrylic / canvas
51 x 66 cm
Collection: Barbara McLeod

the quilt spoke volumes. I was saddened to see they had received so little recognition for their contribution to the development of agriculture in the valley. This was not a deliberate snub. It was just the way things were in the first half of the twentieth century. One small northern community divided by cultural differences from across the Atlantic Ocean.

This simple quilt evoked stories I had long forgotten. As I admired the quilt, I remembered the fortitude of the Ukrainian women who had toiled in the fields of Alberta.

The story of a young Ukrainian girl named Elizabeth Paraska Makarenko came to mind. Her family lived in the war-torn Balkans of eastern Europe. In the first decade of the 1900s, her parents, fearing for her future, placed a name and destination tag around her neck. They kissed her goodbye, knowing they would never see her again, and sent her on a journey halfway around the world. After weeks of travel, knowing no language except her native tongue, she found herself at a railway station in Alberta. Her brothers met her and quickly married her off to a man many years her senior. She moved with her new husband and his children to an isolated homestead and started a new life. She was fifteen.

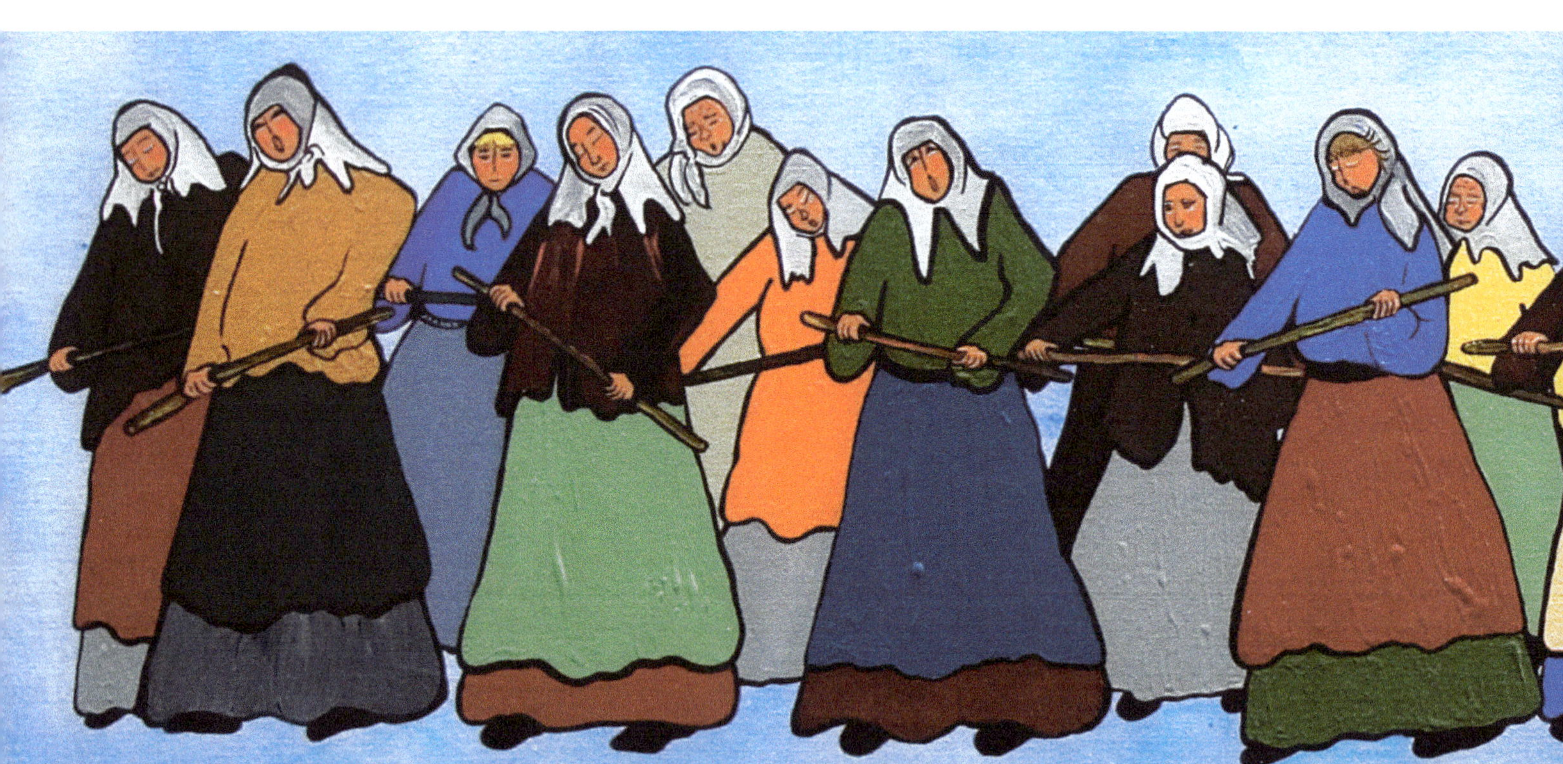

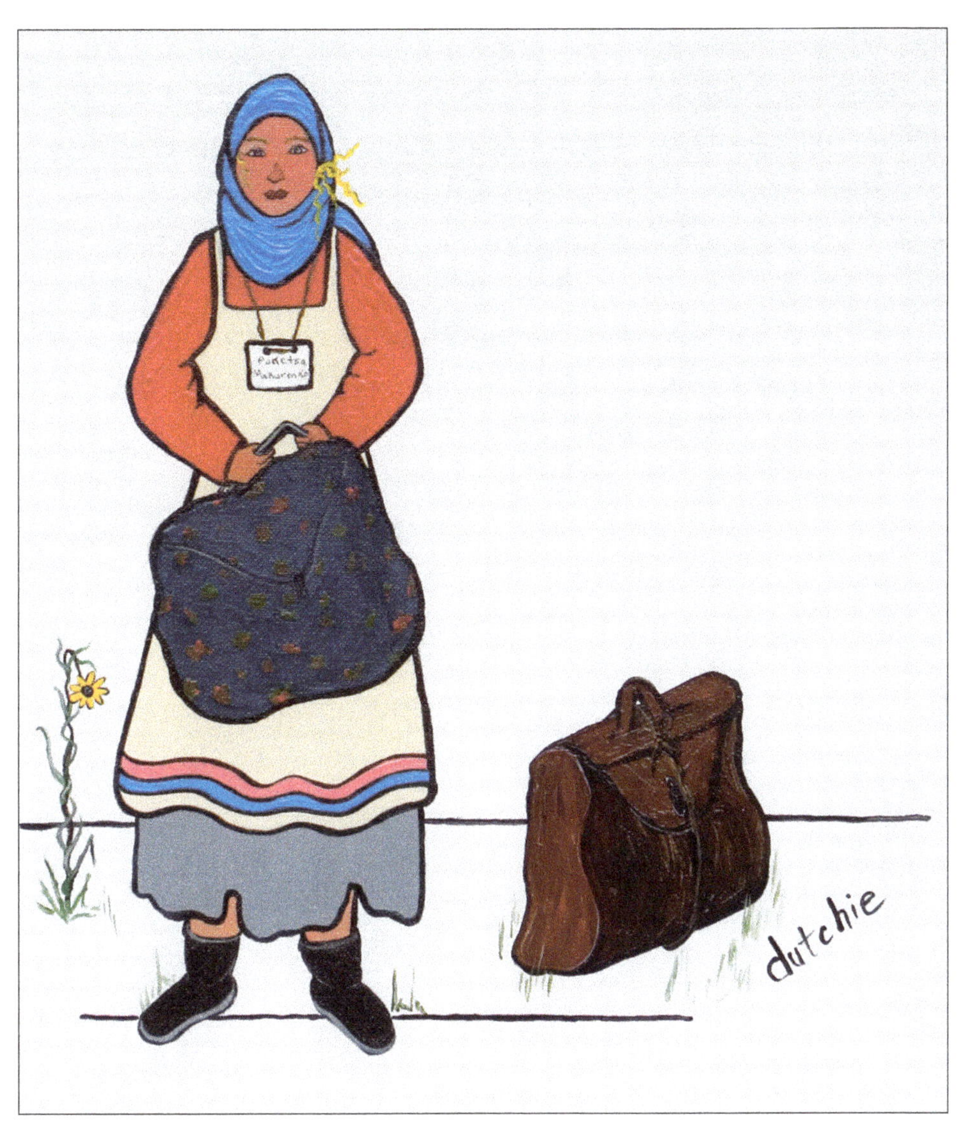

Paraska – Prairie Flower

acrylic / canvas

36 x 41 cm

Collection: Catherine and Bill Cherlenko

Spirit Wrestlers

acrylic / canvas

46 x 147 cm

Collection: Polly Di Clemente (nee Soponoff)

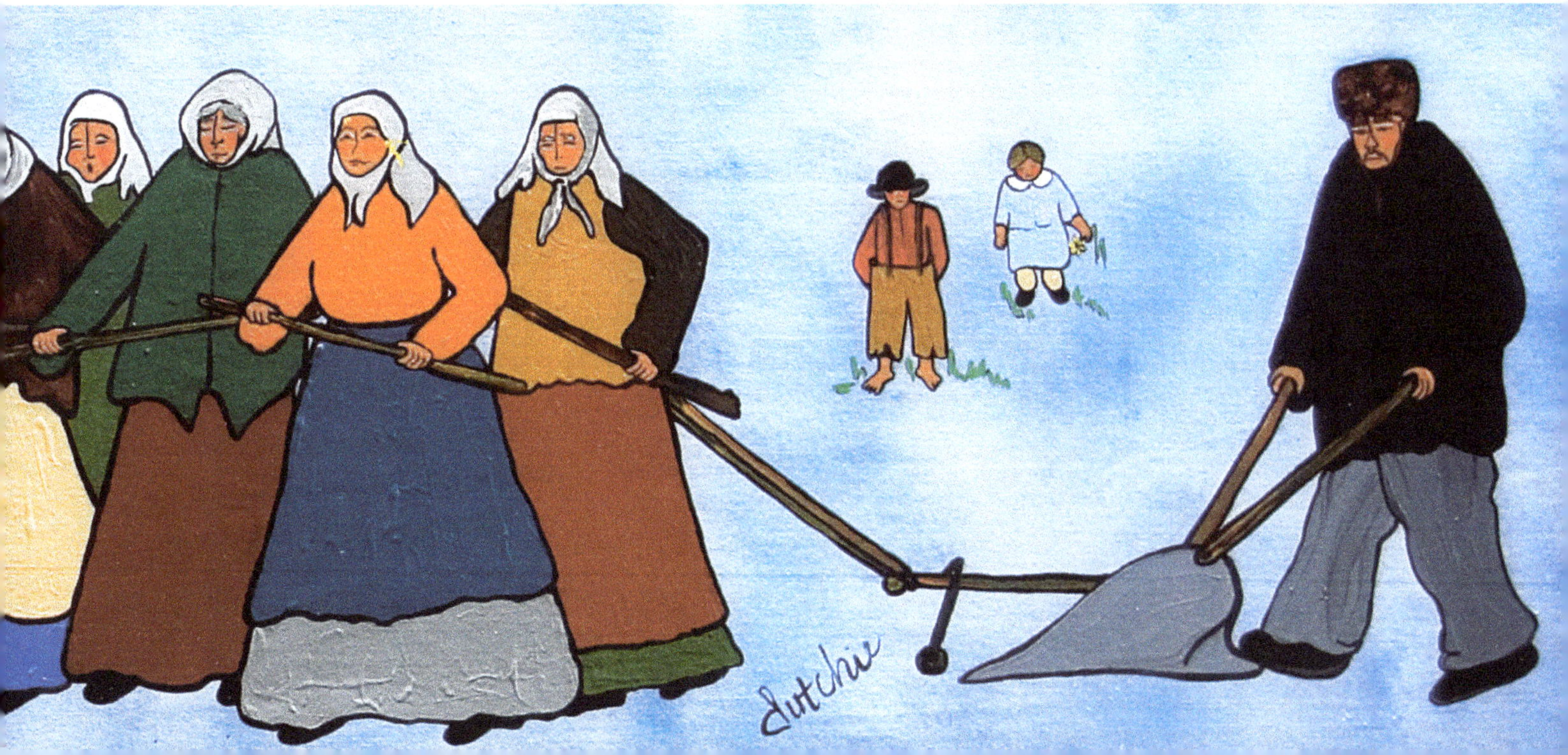

When I painted *Prairie Flower...Bill's Grandmother* I tried to imagine how alone Paraska must have felt. Unable to speak any language but her own, the vastness of the land — what did her future hold?

I wanted to show her loneliness as she waited at the station, as well as the dignity and courage she must have had to make such a journey. Paraska is gone now. How I hope she found happiness.

Ukrainian women were admired by the community at large for their willingness to work in the fields in what was considered men's work by the western European settlers. The admiration, though, was always tinged with an attitude of superiority. "What kind of man would let his wife toil in the fields like an animal?" and "Why would any lady let herself be treated in this manner?" Daughters were warned, "Don't marry a 'Bohunk.' They treat their cows better than they do their wives." And so went the stories of misunderstanding.

Polly, the granddaughter of western Russian settlers, and I spoke at length about the role of women in the farming community during the first half of the twentieth century. She told me how her father and many of the young men had to seek work away from their farms in order to earn money for their families. This left the women and old men to develop the land. No young men. No money. No horse or oxen to pull the plow. As the women gathered and hooked themselves to a breaking plow to turn the virgin earth, they saw it not as servitude, but simply as something that had to be done.

Polly stressed that while her parents had found new land, they held fast to old country values. The emotional struggle, she added, was much more difficult than the labor as a new generation of Canadian children struggled to find their niche in the community without alienating themselves from their families.

The paintings *Spirit Wrestlers* and *Peter 1916* celebrate the lives of Polly's grandmother, her mother and

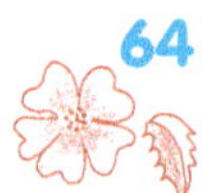

father, and all Russian settlers who found a new home in the valley.

I continued to stand in front of the coverlet with the boldly printed "Please Do Not Touch" sign by its side. When I thought no one was looking I softly traced the letters in Mom's name with my fingers. God, how I missed her at that moment. And I felt more than a little angry that simple thread should have a longer life than that of such a wonderful woman.

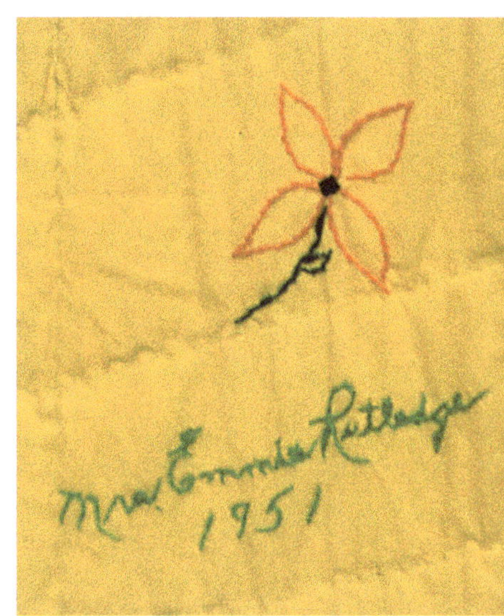

The quilt is symbolic of the contribution valley women made to the development of northern farmlands. Their names deserve to be there. My fingers remember the feel of Mom's name on old cotton. I feel proud, honored. I only wish that the names of all the mothers who homesteaded in the area had their names embroidered on a quilt hanging on a wall in the Kinusayo Museum.

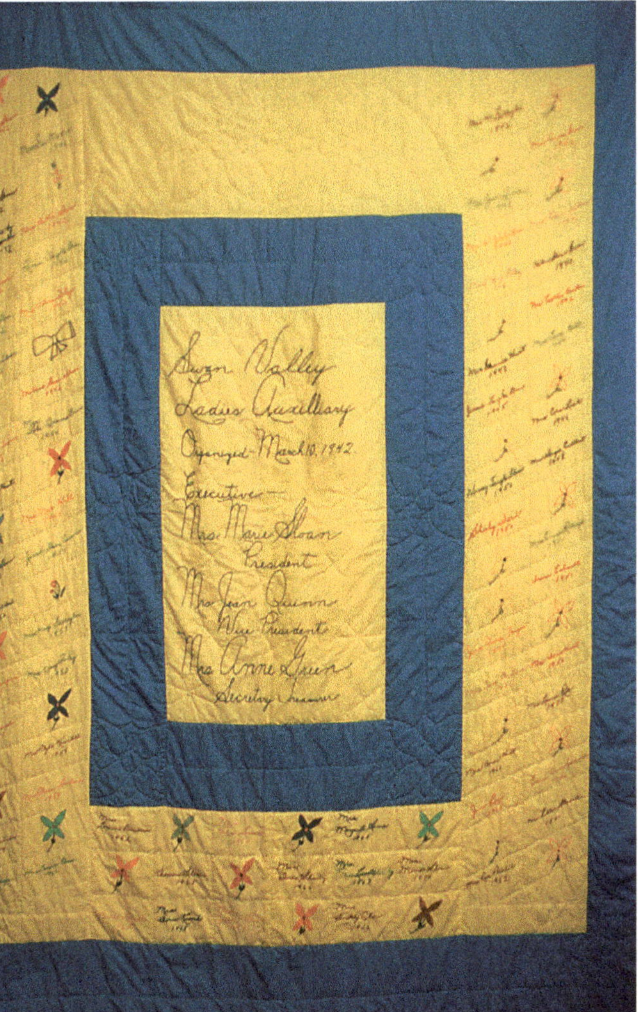

The farming community of my valley is now united. Prejudice has been erased by time and understanding. The farmers prosper. None more so than the ancestors of the Ukrainian homesteaders who came to the valley over a century ago.

Mom's Quilt

Collection: Kinusayo Museum

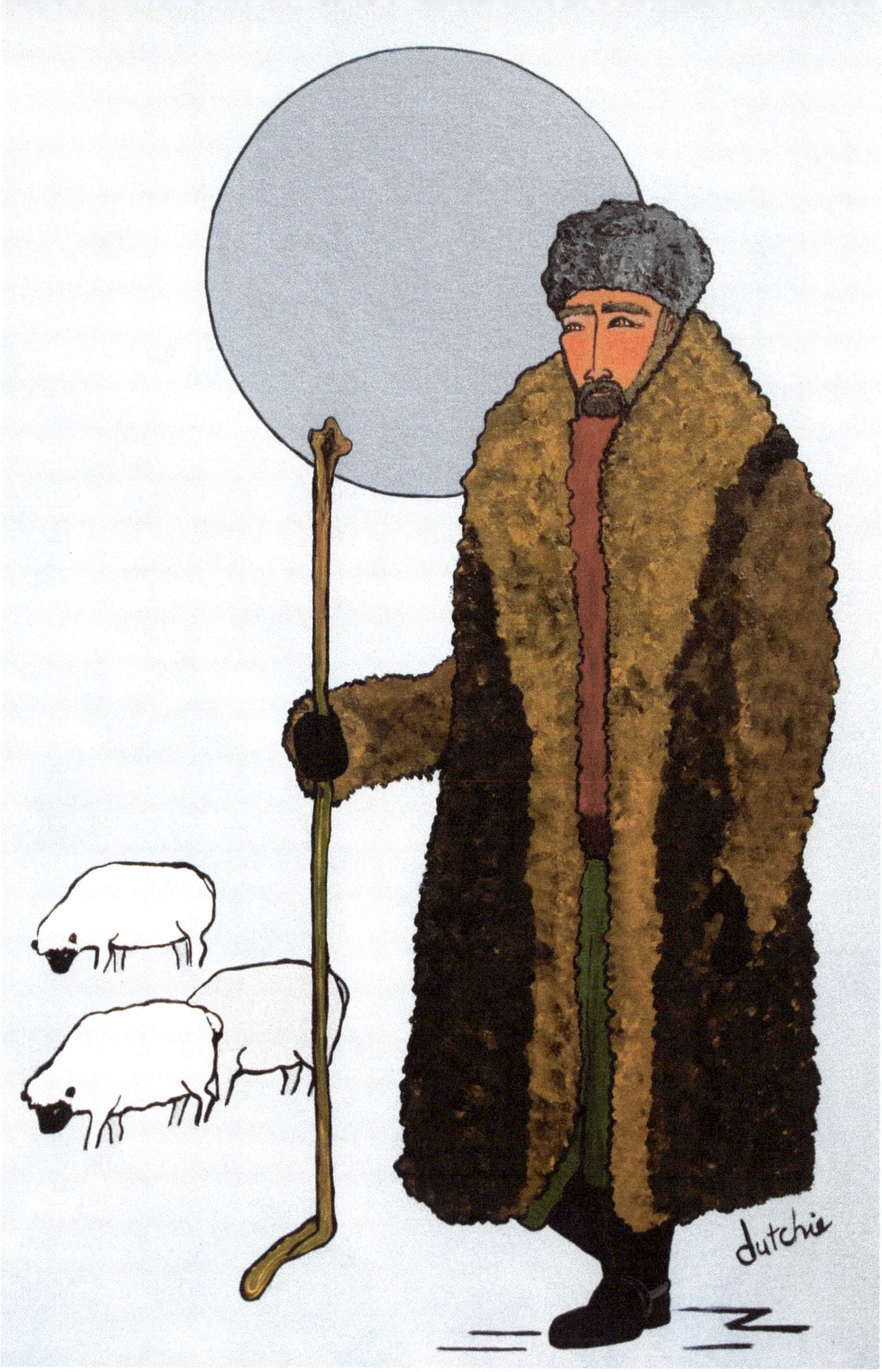

Peter 1916

acrylic / canvas

60 x 91 cm

Collection: Polly Di Clemente (nee Soponoff)

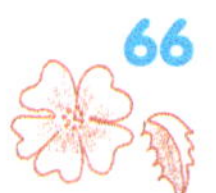

Conclusion

This book was meant to give a quick peek into the daily lives of northern homesteaders at the turn of the twentieth century. If it has done that, I am grateful.

I am going to end my narrative with two more pictures: *Pride for a Job Well Done* and *December*.

When I was at university my friend would dismiss my opinion, if she didn't agree with me, with a loud, "My God, dutchie, you still have one foot in the furrow!"

I thanked her for the compliment…

Today I would add, "and wasn't I lucky."

I was lucky to have had the opportunity to watch my dad at the end of a long day stand and look over his fields. In the spring, after the planting was finished, he would pick up a handful of soil, rub it gently between his fingers. "Good earth," he would say. "This is good earth."

At harvest time he would take a grain head in his hand, rub it gently and blow the chaff into the wind. Slowly he would caress the seeds, place them in his mouth and savor the results of spring's labor. "Good earth," he would say. "This is good earth". I felt his pride in a job well done.

I was lucky. I learned to be proud of who I was and who I am: a homesteader's daughter.

December shows an old man in the December of his life. Like an old tamarack tree, he is stooped and gnarled with time. I placed mining equipment in his hand because I believe that no matter the season of our lives,

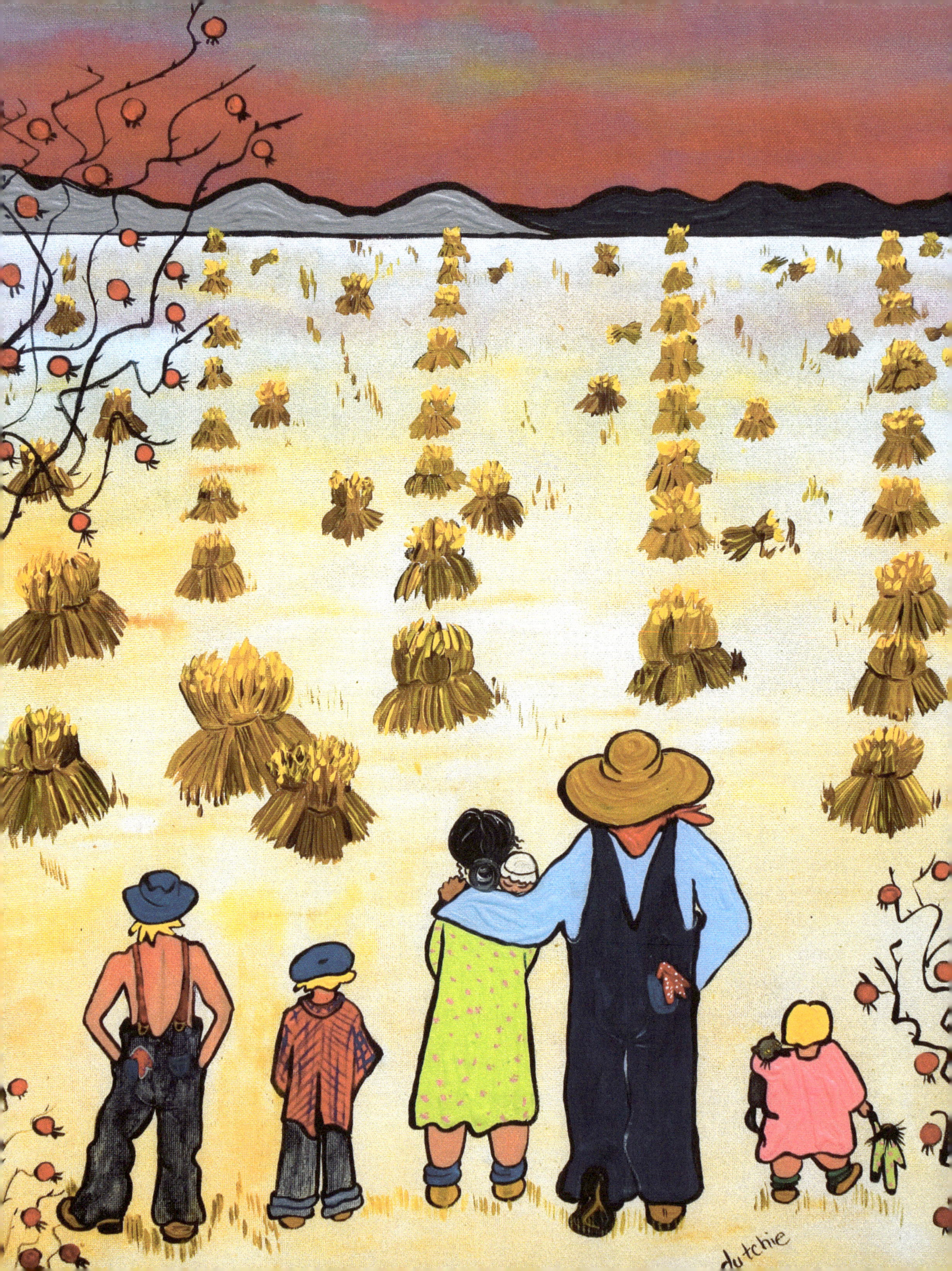
dutchie

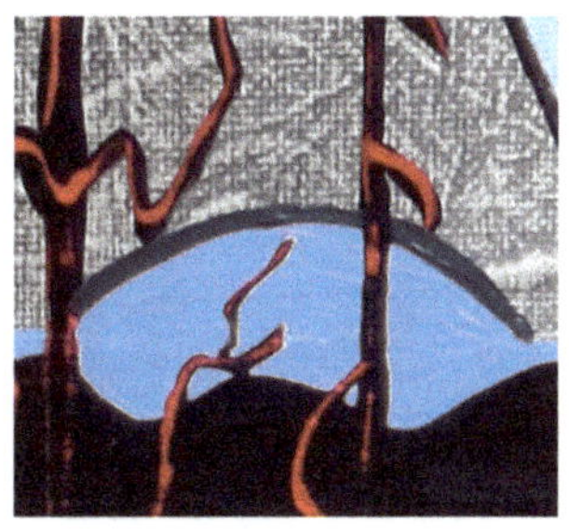

the quest for that proverbial pot of gold lingers in the hearts of all men.

I know that was true of the homestead spirit. Against great odds, men and women from many parts of the world set out on a journey. They were determined to make better lives for themselves and their children. They succeeded. I am proud to have shared their dream.

The season of homesteading is past. I hope that my stories have touched your hearts as they did our Andy's, and that this book will help keep a wonderful time in our history alive.

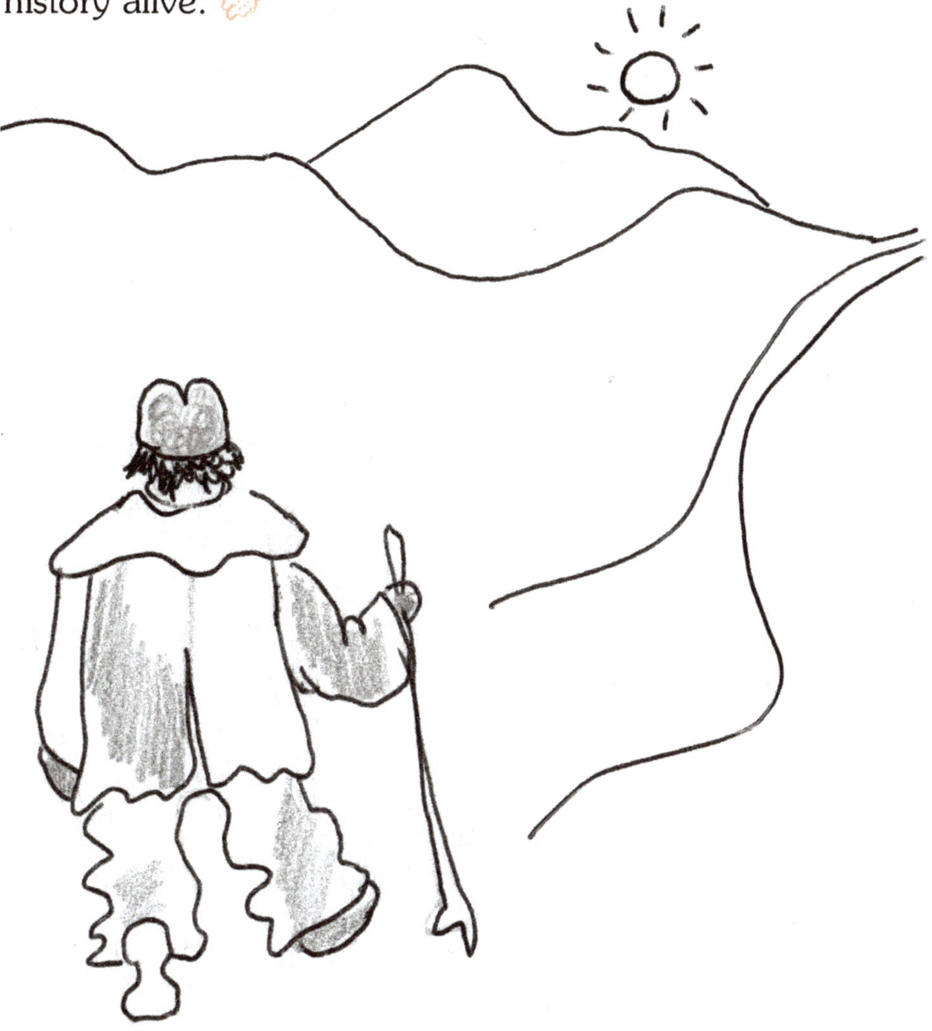

OPPOSITE:

Pride for a Job Well Done

acrylic / canvas

51 x 66 cm

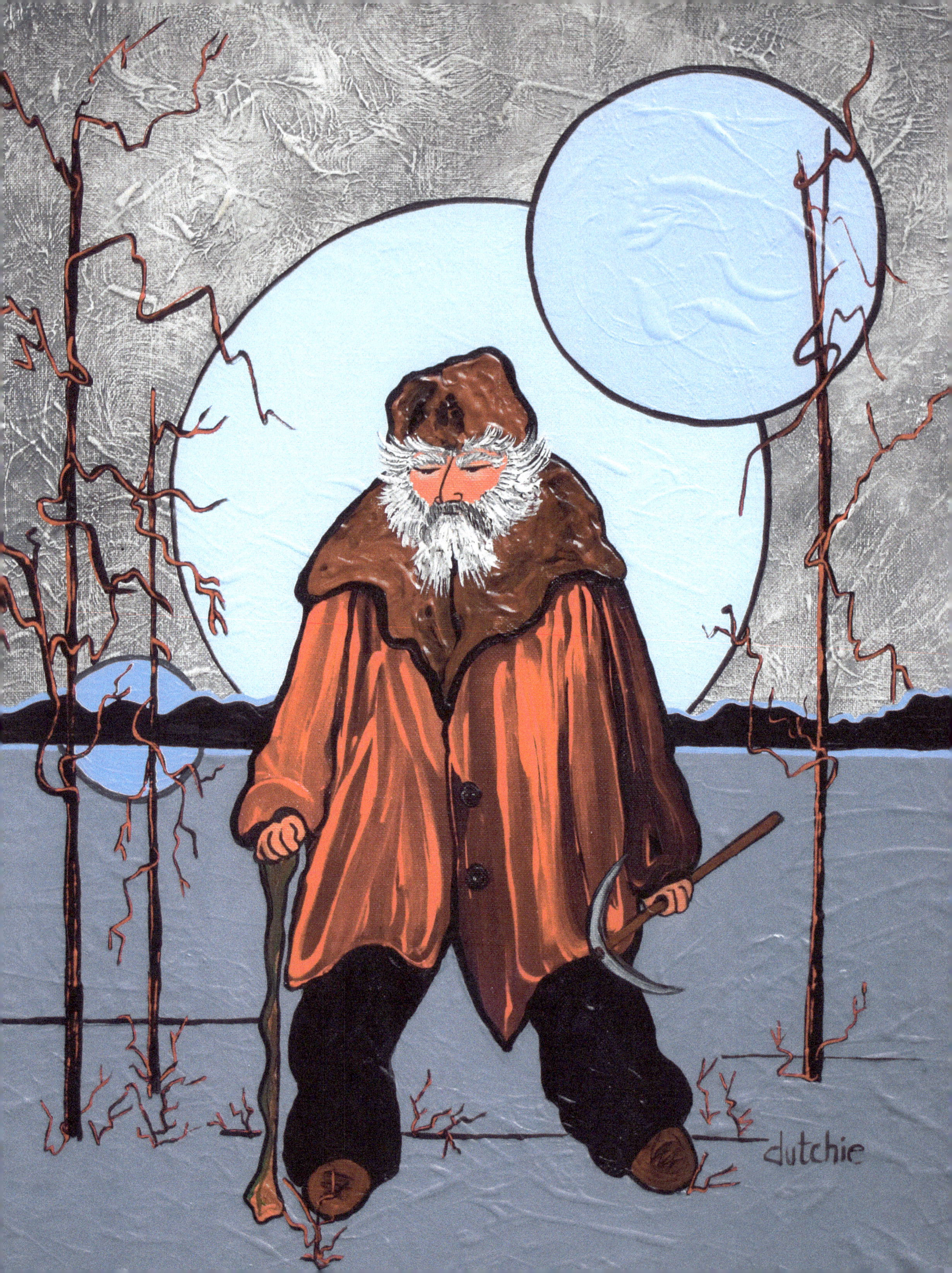
dutchie

Epilogue

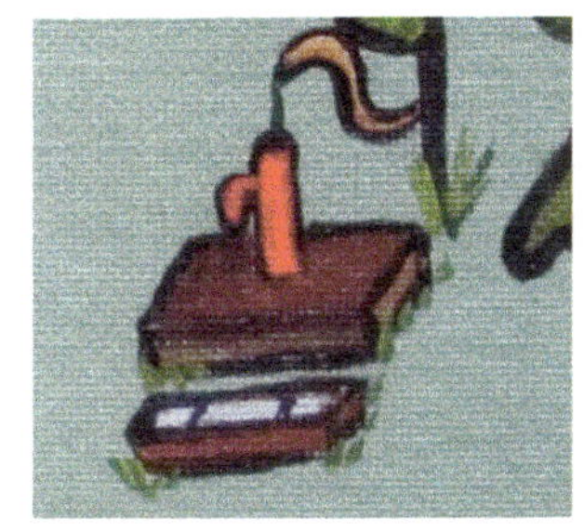

Dear Readers,

Every once in a while we receive an unexpected gift. Mine was finding that small black and white picture of Mom and other ladies from the Valley of the Swan.

It was like receiving one last hug from a much-loved mom.

I started to paint. I could not stop. Into the night old memories emerged on canvas. I didn't give much thought to the creative process. The stories simply flowed forth. I wanted to tell them all. I was possessed.

Memories. Ha! Scorned by youth, revered and exaggerated by the aged. What a fountain of knowledge only to fade away with an aging brain.

I am thankful my memories surfaced and found an outlet before they, too, fell victim to the ravages of time. They restored my soul. Anger was washed away with paint thinner. Happiness came out in the brightest of colors.

I am a lucky woman. I am at peace with my childhood.

My love,
dutchie

OPPOSITE:
December
acrylic / canvas
65 x 51 cm
Collection: Janet and John McLaughlin

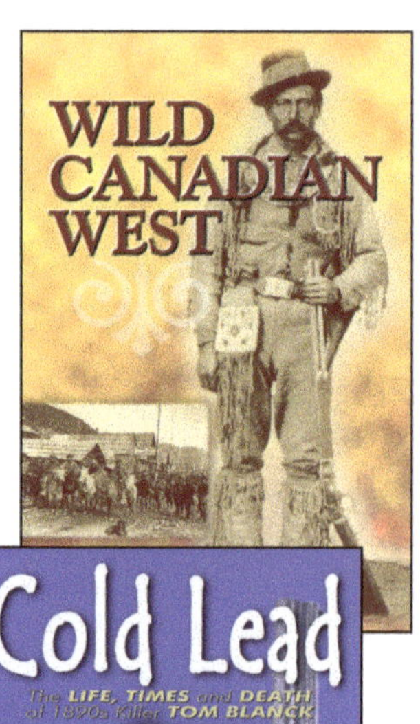

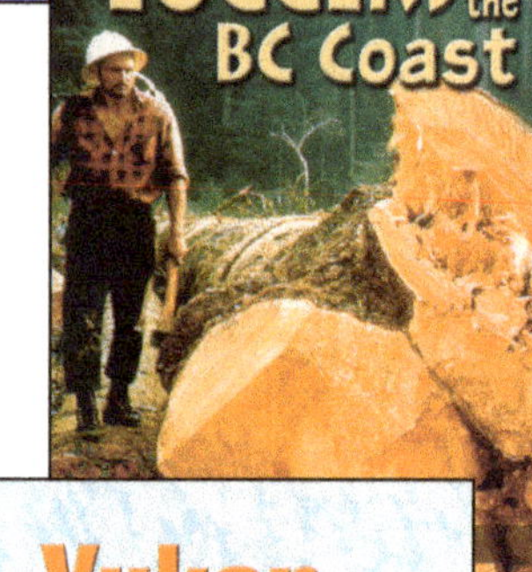

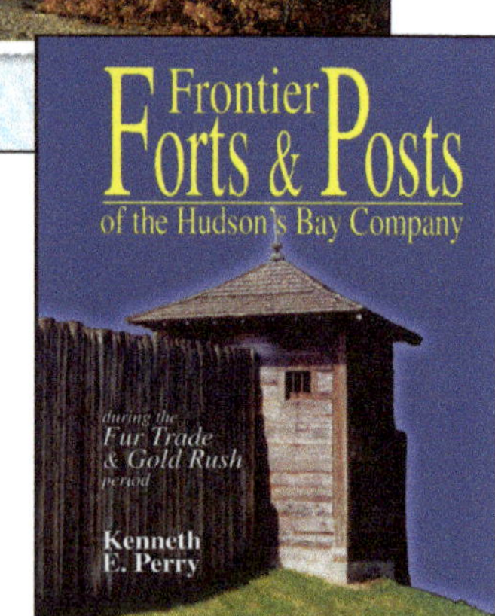

More HANCOCK HOUSE *history & biography titles*

Afloat in Time
Jim Sirois
ISBN 0-88839-455-1
5.5 x 8.5 • sc • 288 pages

Alaska in the Wake of the North Star
Loel Shuler
ISBN 0-88839-587-6
5.5 x 8.5 • sc • 224 pages

Buffalo People
Mildred Valley Thornton
ISBN 0-88839-479-9
5.5 x 8.5 • sc • 208 pp.

Captain McNeill and His Wife the Nishga Chief
Robin Percival Smith
ISBN 0-88839-472-1
5.5 x 8.5 • sc • 256 pages

Cold Lead
Mark Dugan
ISBN 0-88839-559-0
5.5 x 8.5 • sc • 176 pages

Crazy Cooks & Gold Miners
Joyce Yardley
ISBN 0-88839-294-X
5.5 x 8.5 • sc • 224 pages

Crooked River Rats
Bernard McKay
ISBN 0-88839-451-9
5.5 x 8.5 • sc • 176 pages

Deadman's Clothes
Dale Davidson
ISBN 0-88839-608-2
5.5 x 8.5 • sc • 144 pages

Fogswamp
Trudy Turner, Ruth McVeigh
ISBN 0-88839-104-8
5.5 x 8.5 • sc • 255 pages

Frontier Forts & Posts of the Hudson's Bay Co.
Kenneth E. Perry
ISBN 0-88839-598-1
8.5 x 11 • sc • 96 pages

Incredible Gang Ranch
Dale Alsager
ISBN 0-88839-211-7
5.5 x 8.5 • sc • 448 pages

Klondike Paradise
C.R. Porter
ISBN 0-88839-402-0
8.5 x 11 • sc • 176 pages

Lady Rancher
Gertrude Minor Roger
ISBN 0-88839-099-8
5.5 x 8.5 • sc • 184 pages

Lewis & Clark Across the Northwest
Cheryll Halsey
ISBN 0-88839-560-4
5.5 x 8.5 • sc • 112 pages

Loggers of the BC Coast
Hans Knapp
ISBN 0-88839-588-4
5.5 x 8.5 • sc • 200 pages

Nahanni Trailhead
Joanne Ronan Moore
ISBN 0-88839-464-0
5.5 x 8.5 • sc • 256 pages

Out of the Rain
Paul Jones
ISBN 0-88839-541-8
5.5 x 8.5 • sc • 272 pages

Outposts & Bushplanes
Bruce Lamb
ISBN 0-88839-556-6
5.5 x 8.5 • sc • 208 pages

Potlatch People
Mildred Valley Thornton
ISBN 0-88839-491-8
5.5 x 8.5 • sc • 320 pages

Puffin Cove
Neil Carey
ISBN 0-88839-216-8
5.5 x 8.5 • sc • 178 pages

Ralph Edwards of Lonesome Lake
Ed Gould
ISBN 0-88839-100-5
5.5 x 8.5 • sc • 296 pages

Raven and the Mountaineer
Monty Alford
ISBN 0-88839-542-6
5.5 x 8.5 • sc • 152 pages

Rivers of Gold
Gwen & Don Lee
ISBN 0-88839-555-8
5.5 x 8.5 • sc • 204 pages

Ruffles on my Longjohns
Isabel Edwards
ISBN 0-88839-102-1
5.5 x 8.5 • sc • 297 pages

Timeless Trails of the Yukon
Dolores Cline Brown
ISBN 0-88839-584-5
5.5 x 8.5 • sc • 184 pages

Walter Moberly and the Northwest Passage by Rail
Daphne Sleigh
ISBN 0-88839-510-8
5.5 x 8.5 • sc • 272 pages

Wild Trails, Wild Tales
Bernard McKay
ISBN 0-88839-395-4
5.5 x 8.5 • sc • 176 pages

Wild Canadian West
E. C. (Ted) Meyers
ISBN 0-88839-469-1
5.5 x 8.5 • sc • 208 pages

Yukon Riverboat Days
Joyce Yardley
ISBN 0-88839-386-5
5.5 x 8.5 • sc • 176 pages

Yukon Tears and Laughter
Joyce Yardley
ISBN 0-88839-594-9
5.5 x 8.5 • sc • 176 pages

Yukoners: True Tales
H. Gordon-Cooper
ISBN 0-88839-232-X
5.5 x 8.5 • sc • 144 pages

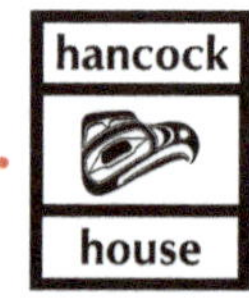

View all HANCOCK HOUSE *titles at* **www.hancockhouse.com**

www.ingramcontent.com/pod-product-compliance
Lightning Source LLC
LaVergne TN
LVHW060642110826
845147LV00018B/1023
9780888396259